Fabulous
PLAY
HOUSE
PLANS

Simple and Sophisticated Hideaways for Boys and Girls

Kathy Smith Anthenat

BETTERWAY BOOKS
Cincinnati, Ohio

Also by Kathy Smith Anthenat
American Tree Houses and Play Houses

Fabulous Play House Plans. Copyright © 1993 by Kathy Smith Anthenat. Printed and bound in the United States of America. All rights reserved. No part of this book may be reproduced in any form or by any electronic or mechanical means including information storage and retrieval systems without permission in writing from the publisher, except by a reviewer, who may quote brief passages in a review. Published by Betterway Books, an imprint of F&W Publications, Inc., 1507 Dana Avenue, Cincinnati, Ohio 45207. 1-800-289-0963. First edition.

97 96 95 94 93   5 4 3 2 1

Library of Congress Cataloging-in-Publication Data

Anthenat, Kathy Smith, 1953-
    Fabulous play house plans: simple and sophisticated hideaways for boys and girls / Kathy Smith Anthenat. — 1st ed.
        p.   cm.
    Includes index.
    ISBN 1-55870-283-0: $16.95
    1. Playhouses, Children's — Design and construction — Amateurs' manuals. 2. Playhouses, Children's — Designs and plans. I. Title.
    TH4967.A58   1993
    690'.89 — dc20   92-35276
                                                CIP

To Bruce,
for having faith in my abilities
and teaching me to also.

Acknowledgments

I am greatly indebted to the following people for their help in brainstorming ideas, providing information or plans, allowing me to include their designs, or acting as models for this book.

Little Red Schoolhouse: Heather Goodman

Fairy Princess Play House: Caitlin Meyers

Combination Log Cabin Play House/Storage Shed: Bruce Anthenat, Alan and Kelly Anthenat

Colonial Dollhouse/Play House: Ken Manda Builders, Ken B. Manda, Ken M. and Matthew Manda

Cardboard Castle: Patrick and Douglas Klatskin, Kelly and Alan Anthenat

Office Skyscraper: Lonnie Ross

Heather's Hideaway: Jeff Short, Heather and J.J. Short

Cheshire Cat Play House: Southern Forest Products Association, Richard Wallace

Victorian Play House: Bruce Anthenat, Kelly Anthenat

Tepee: Bruce Anthenat, Alan and Kelly Anthenat

Lean-To: Bruce Anthenat, Alan Anthenat

Southern Pine Play House: Southern Forest Products Association, Richard Wallace

Tourist Cabin: University of Tennessee Agricultural Extension Service, George F. Grandle

Four Person Tourist Cabin: University of Tennessee Agricultural Extension Service, George F. Grandle

PVC Pipe Play House: Kelly Anthenat, Sara, Todd, and Jayne Layman

Homewise Play House/Storage Shed: Homewise, Inc., Al Wasco, Jim LaRue

Dowel Doodles Play House: Alan Anthenat

24' A-Frame Cabin: U.S. Department of Agriculture, Purdue University

APA Three-Stage Cabin: American Plywood Association, Mick Shultz

Lofty Lookout: Tom Kauffman

Buckeye Trading Post: Bruce Anthenat, Christopher Meyers

Caitlin's Castle: Michael Pascucci, Caitlin Pascucci

All-American Play House: Dale Szarka, Brent Szarka

Clubhouse/Garden Shed: John D. Lowood, MacMillan Bloedel/Structural Board Association

Preface

There is something very soul-satisfying about building a play house, whether you are doing it as a child or as an adult. What a wonderful way to express your creativity and skill! As the structure begins to take shape you step back and view your progress; pride swells in your chest—a sense of accomplishment that plunking down money at a cash register for a factory-made, molded plastic play house will never give you.

This book contains a variety of play house styles in order to broaden your ideas about what a play house should look like. The plans are small, but I wanted to include as many plans as possible to provide you with many choices. Since most parents will not build all of the play houses included, the expense of reproducing the plans for the play house(s) of your choice is nominal. I suggest taking the book to your local copy store and copying the plans for your choice at 200%. This will make all of the markings easy to read and to understand. All of the full size patterns are reproduced here at full size.

It was necessary to reduce the plans considerably in order to include the variety you see in the book. The building materials include wood, PVC pipe, fabric, wire, grass, and cardboard. My goal is to inspire children and adults to discover—or improve—their skills as they create a special little retreat and another wonderful childhood memory.

Contents

Some Notes About Play Houses

Constructing a play house for a child is one of the most all-around pleasurable projects that a parent or grandparent can work on. There are so many options to choose from: How big? What kind? Where should we put it? Planning is half the fun of this kind of project, so take your time and browse through this book and your mind for ideas. Here are some things to consider.

LOCATION

Will it be an indoor play house, an outdoor play house, or both?

Inside

An indoor play house is a real treat for children if you have the space for one. Play houses reduce adult-size rooms into child-size spaces. Be sure that what you have in mind will fit in your house—low enough for the ceilings and narrow enough for the doorways, or able to be disassembled. If a playhouse is narrow enough to fit through the doorway and low enough for the ceilings, it can be tipped over if necessary to move it through the doorway. The Little Red Schoolhouse (page 17) is 7'3" tall, short enough to fit under standard eight-foot-high ceilings. Because it is too wide to fit through standard household doorways, it is specifically designed in take-apart sections and can be reassembled easily in the desired location. On the other hand, since the frame for the Fairy Princess Play House (page 27) is small enough to fit through most doorways, it is permanently cemented together. Play houses that are lightweight enough can be carried out to the patio so that your children can enjoy fresh air and sunshine on warm, sunny days.

Outside

If you are planning an outdoor play house, will it have windows and doors to keep out rain and snow, or just window and door openings? If you plan to use windows, ones that can be opened are preferable. The midday sun can quickly heat up a play house that isn't well-ventilated. Inexpensive, screened, double-hung storm windows can be opened to prevent your creation from becoming a hot box in which no child wants to play. Often you can buy used regular windows for just a few dollars, or get them free from someone who is remodeling a house and putting in new windows.

If you are planning a permanent outdoor play house, where in the yard will it be located? Choose the location carefully if you are building a permanent outdoor play house. Do you want it close to the house where it is easier for the parent or caregiver to keep an eye on young children, or do you want it located on the back edge of the property to give the children more privacy and keep the noise away from the house? If you are building an elaborate structure such as the Victorian Play House, you might want to position it to be the focal point of your backyard landscaping scheme. If the play house will eventually become a guest cottage or a home office, do you want to have room to make a driveway to it later?

Take sun, wind, and shade patterns into account when choosing a location. For instance, children love watching things grow and you might want to let them have a small flower or vegetable garden next to the play house. If so, make sure the play house will not be blocking sunlight from the growing plants.

When possible, the back of the play house should be facing the direction of prevailing winds to help prevent rain and snow from being blown in through the doorway during storms. Also, remember that the hot sun can heat a metal slide to an unusable temperature in the middle of the day during the summer. If you plan to include a metal slide, you can minimize this problem by facing the sliding surface toward the north. Fiberglass slides are now available; they eliminate the heat problem.

DURABILITY

How long do you want the play house to last?

Disposable

If you are looking for ideas for an inexpensive, disposable play house, consider the old standby — cardboard boxes obtained for free from a furniture or appliance store. Three examples are included here: Sunshine and Flowers Cottage (page 43), Cardboard Castle (page 46), and Office Skyscraper (page 48). As these three illustrate, a cardboard play house can be as plain or fancy as you want to make it. A coat or two of paint will make them more durable and will also dull sharp edges, making paper cuts to small fingers less likely.

One tip about working with cardboard: If you are cutting out windows or doors and the box bends somewhere you don't want a bend, reinforce the box by gluing a scrap of cardboard to the interior side of that area for added strength that doesn't show.

Permanent

Usually the more durable a structure is, the more expensive it is also. Treated wood will last longer than untreated wood — and also cost more. If your family moves around a lot you are probably not interested in a permanent structure; it will break your child's heart to leave it behind the next time you move. However, if you are as certain as anyone can be of staying right where you are for many years to come, permanent play houses such as Heather's Hideaway (page 51) and the Victorian Play House (page 64) will still be there to entertain the next generation of children.

PORTABILITY

Will your play house be portable?

Do you want to be able to move it to mow the yard or relocate it from the living room to the basement? One advantage of this feature is that if you have very small children, you can move the play house to where you can keep an eye on them while working or relaxing. The PVC Pipe Play House (page 89) can be used as a portable sunshade for a baby's play pen by the pool, the garden, or wherever. The Dowel Doodles Play House (page 103) is not only portable but also compact enough when disassembled to store on a shelf in the closet or to take to Grandma's house.

MATERIALS

What materials will be used to make it?

Be creative! Improvise. Innovate. Consider all the possibilities: finished lumber, rough cut lumber, saplings from your woods, landscape timbers, used telephone poles, used fencing, redwood, lattice panels, paper, cardboard, canvas, fabric, fiberglass panels, acrylic sheets, metal pipe, PVC pipe, tires and other recycled materials, adobe brick, wood shingles, pegboard, cork, hardboard, plywood, grass bundles, glass blocks, concrete blocks, brick, wire fence, etc. Browse through your local building supply, fabric, and craft stores. Take notice when you see people throwing away usable building supplies because they are doing some remodeling.

Look at what other people are using. One easy

Create a People Play House at your child's next birthday party. First, construct a cube-shaped frame from PVC pipe and fittings; the height depends on the height of the children. Next, cover the top with balloons for a colorful roof. As the children arrive for the party, they make the "People" walls by lying down on a strip of white paper and having someone else trace their outline. (Be sure they have their arms stretched upwards.) The children color in the outlines, cut them out, and hang them on the frame. If there are a lot of children, hang some of the outlines facing outward and some facing inward.

way to do this is to flip through a copy of *American Tree Houses and Play Houses* (Betterway Publications, 1991). This book contains a large collection of photographs of current and historical play houses.

Look at new ways to use everyday things. Those brown paper sacks you carried groceries home in would be great for making a papier-mâché cave or igloo, or even a gingerbread house trimmed with colorful, painted, papier-mâché candy. Use the long cardboard tubes that carpeting is rolled on to make the walls of a tropical island hut; the grass roof could be made from strips of green crêpe paper.

Don't forget about nature when brainstorming for ideas for play houses. Tie several tall poles together at the top like a tepee, leaving an opening on one side for a doorway. Plant pole bean or morning-glory seeds (or any fast-growing, climbing plant) at the base of each pole. Your son or daughter will have the fun of watching the walls of the "play house" grow higher and higher.

APPEARANCE

Will the play house imitate something else?

Some play houses are purposely very plain so that they become whatever a child's imagination makes them each day. Four walls can become a fort one day and a fire station the next. Other play houses are designed to imitate a building—a schoolhouse, castle, or general store. Sometimes they imitate a form of transportation—a covered wagon, boat, or spaceship. Still others imitate the exterior appearance of the family home. These types of theme play houses can be a lot of fun to construct and to equip. You could put school desks and a blackboard in a schoolhouse, for example.

ELEVATION

Will it be a ground level play house or an elevated one?

Ground level play houses are safer for very young children. Elevated play houses include the added fun of deciding how to get up and down, and kids—who spend much of their time looking up at adults—enjoy the opportunity to look down at them from a lofty perch. Let your children help decide between the choices available for ascent and descent: wood ladder, rope or chain ladder, knotted rope, slide, ramp, climbing net, "string" of attached tires, stairway, or fireman's pole.

SIZE

How big will the play house be?

There are several things to keep in mind when deciding how big to make a play house: How many months or years do I want my child to be able to use this play house? How much space do I have—indoors or outdoors—for one? Do I want my child to be able to lie down inside it (for instance, for taking a nap)? Should the floor area inside be large enough for sleepovers? How big a play house can I afford? Does my child prefer spacious or cozy play areas?

If you do want your children to be able to have sleepovers in the play house, figure that a youth's sleeping bag is about 27″ × 60″ and an adult's sleeping

This little princess is standing in a lofty tower overlooking her backyard kingdom. Tomorrow her imagination may transform the play structure into a ship's bridge or an airport control tower.

bag is about 33″ × 78″. You will need a minimum of two sleeping bag spaces.

To help you decide how tall to make doorways and ceilings, the approximate heights of children at each age are listed below:

2 years old — 2′10″
3 years old — 3′2″
4 years old — 3′5″
5 years old — 3′8″
6 years old — 3′11″
7 years old — 4′2 ″
8 years old — 4′4″
9 years old — 4′6″
10 years old — 4′8″
11 years old — 4′11″
12 years old — 5′1″
13 years old — you might as well make it tall enough for an adult!

PURPOSE

Do you want the structure to serve more than one purpose?

Play houses can be combined with other structures for increased usefulness. The Combination Log Cabin Play House/Storage Shed (page 34) includes an enclosed area that can be used to store garden and lawn tools and equipment. Perhaps you want a play house that also includes a pump house for your swimming pool or a dog house for the family pet.

Many people who build outdoor play houses like to use them to store patio furniture during the winter months, but make the doorway too narrow. If you think you might want to use your play house for that purpose, make sure that either the main doorway is wide enough, or there is another wide entrance to the play house — perhaps double doors in the rear or on the side.

Play houses such as the Traditional 8′ × 12′ Play House (page 98) or the Lofty Lookout (page 135) are large enough to use for Scout meetings in addition to daily play, and can eventually be turned into guest cottages or home offices. The 24′ A-Frame Cabin (page 106) can even be turned into rental property or a first home for a grown child. It's a lot of money to spend on a play house, but if you have the space think of how many years of use it will get. When little Billy becomes teenage Billy and his heavy metal rock band needs a place to practice, you may decide that the large play house at the back of the property was one of the best investments you ever made!

CONSTRUCTION

In Stages

Do you want to be able to build the play house in stages?

Some play houses have all or nothing designs; that is, they are not really useful until the entire building is constructed. Others can be built a portion at a time, with each portion serving a purpose by itself. The Combination Log Cabin Play House/Storage Shed, for instance, can start out as just a shaded sandbox with a baby swing hanging from one of the floor joists. You can add the elevated log cabin later when time and money permit, and enclose the storage area

How much your children can help with the construction of a play house depends on their age and past experience. This brother and sister have been helping with family construction projects for several years.

the next year. Or reverse the order and enclose the storage area first and add the log cabin second.

With Children

Do you want the construction of the play house to be a learning experience for your children?

Working on a play house is an ideal way for your children to begin learning how to use a hammer, screwdriver, and paintbrush. Give them guidance and allow them to learn from their own mistakes. The play house will mean a lot more to them if they are allowed to help design and build it. If you are really concerned about the final appearance of the play house, plan ahead; the novelty of painting usually doesn't last very long, so let Johnny smear on the primer coat. You can apply the finish coat. Or let Susy use scraps of wood to make shelves to go between the exposed studs on the inside while you work on the outside. What she does on the inside isn't going to detract from the appearance of your property or the neighborhood, so let her bend a few nails on some crooked shelves. Afterwards, watch her beaming face as she shows off her carpentry skills to friends. That's the stuff wonderful childhood memories are made from.

Building a lean-to will teach a ten-year-old how to make a shelter in the woods with only twine and a

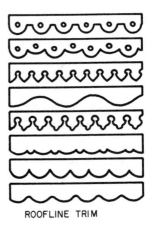

ROOFLINE TRIM

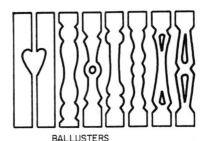

BALLUSTERS

A few decorative boards cut from 1 × 4s can add a lot of charm to otherwise very plain play houses. Shown here are examples of roofline trim styles and baluster shapes for porch railings.

bucksaw. Constructing a grass hut will expose children to a type of home construction used in other cultures, as will a play house made of adobe bricks. Even putting together a Dowel Doodles Play House is a learning experience; you have to plan ahead to get the color pattern you want and to put the doorway in the right spot.

FINISHING DETAILS

What kinds of details will you add?

Will the windows have attached flower boxes on the outside? Or shutters—decorative or working? Would trellises look nice attached on either side of the front door for climbing vines and flowers? Other possible finishing touches are: a child-sized white picket fence, a flagstone path, a mailbox, a name plaque, a welcome mat, indoor or outdoor child-sized furniture, colorful flags and banners waving in the breeze, shelves and bins inside for toys and treasures, a coat rack, curtains, stenciled designs on the walls or floor, a bulletin board or blackboard, a fold-down table to play games on, electricity for lights, and an

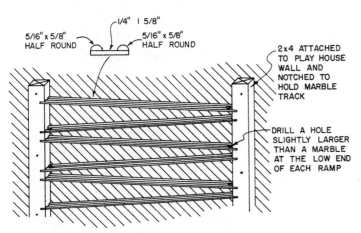

A Marble Track is a fun addition to a play house wall. The ramps are placed at a slight incline; the longer the ramps the better. There is something very soothing about watching the marble and listening to it roll and drop ... roll and drop. Do not drill a hole in the bottom ramp or you will have marbles all over the floor! CAUTION: Do not use the marble track around very small children who may put the marbles in their mouths.

intercom system between the play house and the house.

SAFETY

Appropriate ages are not indicated for any of the play houses included in this book because you are a better judge of your child's abilities than anyone. An unguarded loft edge may be no problem for one child, but may be very dangerous for another child of the same age who has a tendency to fall off things. When in doubt, opt for extra safety features. Keep in mind that your child's friends will also be playing there, and they may not be as safety conscious as your own child.

Wood surfaces should be sanded to prevent splinters. Use a rasp or sandpaper to round off sharp edges or corners on which children might hurt themselves. Be sure there are no protruding nails or bolts to snag clothes on. If you will be using shingles on the roof, make sure the thickness of the plywood and the length of the roofing nails are such that the tips of the nails do not stick out on the underside of the roof.

Buttons should not be used on cloth play houses for toddlers. They can be ripped off and swallowed. Be on the lookout for railings and window holes that a child might get his head or neck stuck in. Small children should never be left unattended while playing, and even older children should be watched for some time when trying out a new play house so that you can remedy any unforeseen problems with the structure.

You should periodically test the structure and any accessories such as climbing ropes, slides, swings, etc., with your own weight. While it is true that your child doesn't weigh as much as you do, each stress point will likely be subjected to the combined weight of several children at times when they are playing.

NOTES

Some of the plans in this book include a Bill of Materials; some do not. Whether or not one is provided, it is best for you to go through the plans and make up your own. Doing so will improve your understanding of the project from the very beginning. You may think of a way to lay out the wood for cutting which will result in less scrap—and less required wood—than another builder. Also, you may already have some building materials left over from other projects which you can use in the play house, or you can make substitutions if you are aware of where each board or piece of hardware is intended to be used.

Some of the plans include step-by-step instructions; others do not—especially the larger play houses. If you have home building experience, the information given for each project will be adequate. If you are a beginning do-it-yourselfer, go to the library and check out a couple of basic home building and carpentry books. What better place to make a few mistakes for the sake of learning than with a play house. You can either correct mistakes or tell the neighbors that it's actually a planned design change!

PART I

Play House Plans

LITTLE RED SCHOOLHOUSE

Designed by Kathy Smith Anthenat

Playing school is a favorite activity of young children, and this play house is just what the teacher ordered! It has a bell in the belfry to ring in the beginning of classes for all those teddy bears and dolls, and the U.S. flag posted at the double front doors. The knotty pine wood floor inside has a stenciled design around the border, and there is plenty of room to attach a blackboard below the large triangular window on the back wall.

The base is approximately 4' × 4', and it is 7'3" to the top of the belfry. Corner braces are used for assembly so that it can be disassembled into eight pieces (front, back, two sides, two roof pieces, floor, and belfry) for moving or storing for the next generation of children. The one pictured cost $325 to build. Although this Little Red Schoolhouse is strictly for indoor use, it wouldn't be hard to revise the plans to use exterior grade building materials if you prefer an outdoor play house.

BILL OF MATERIALS

6 — 4' × 8' sheets ¼" lauan plywood
22 — 1" × 2" × 8'
11 — 8' long ¹¹⁄₁₆" quarter round
17 — 8' long ¾" × ¾" trim
10 — 8' long ¹¹⁄₁₆" × 1¾" trim
2 — 8' long ¼" × ¾" flat screen moulding
12 — 1" corner brace
12 — 1½" corner brace
6 — 1" brass hinge
2 — brass cabinet handles
1 — 8" long ⁷⁄₁₆" diameter wood dowel
bell — approximately 5" diameter
U.S. flag — approximately 8" × 12", on a pole
8 oz. — gray paint
8 oz. — black paint
8 oz. — blue paint
2 quarts — red paint
3 quarts — white paint
1 quart — polyurethane
wood putty
counterweight (for bell assembly)
string or cord, 4'
fasteners:
    wood glue
    flat head screws
    and brads

INSTRUCTIONS

Floor

Construct as shown in FLOOR drawing. Sand top and sides smooth. Use blue paint to stencil the border design (FULL SIZE PATTERN FOR FLOOR DESIGN) on the flat 1 × 2s. Paint the tops of the plywood spacer, the 1 × 2s on edge, and all of the sides, gray. Cover top and sides of entire floor with four coats of polyurethane, sanding lightly between coats.

Front, Back, and Sides

Cut plywood base for each piece using the FRONT PLYWOOD PATTERN, REAR PLYWOOD PATTERN, and SIDE PLYWOOD PATTERN. Draw the guidelines for the siding on the rough side of the plywood; the smooth side will be the interior wall. (Hint: Drill a large hole in each window for a place to start the jigsaw blade.)

Attach trim to rough side as illustrated in FRONT TRIM, SIDE TRIM, and DETAILS A, B, C, and D. The trim for the back panel is the same as for the front panel on the top and sides. Outline the triangular window with ¾ × ¾ trim. The interior edges of the trim should be flush with the edges of the window openings. Be sure the quarter round on the interior side is firmly attached; this "baseboard" will set on top of the play house floor and carry the weight of the house.

Cut 3" wide strips of plywood for siding and attach using brads and glue. The siding will overlap ½". Note: Before cutting these strips it would be best to cut the remaining pieces of plywood needed for the roof, belfry, doors, and sign. Anything remaining can then be cut into 3" wide strips as needed.

Paint interior sides of the panels and all trim white. Paint siding red.

Assemble the panels on the play house floor (the bottom quarter round sits on the floor) with 1½" corner braces — three at each corner.

Make a flag support out of a small piece of 1 × 2 or ¹¹⁄₁₆ × 1¾ by rounding the corners and drilling a hole in the center of it — a little larger than the flag pole and at an angle so that the flag is held at an angle when mounted. Attach flag support to front of schoolhouse and paint blue.

Roof

Cut plywood for roof as shown in ROOF drawing. Attach trim.

Place the two roof panels on top of the schoolhouse. Cut two peak supports using FULL SIZE PATTERN FOR PEAK SUPPORT and four peak braces as shown in PEAK BRACE drawing. Attach to interior side of roof as shown in ROOF DETAIL.

Remove roof panels; paint interior side and trim white. Give the exterior side a textured look by first painting white, then dabbing it with the end of a paint brush—first with gray, then black, then very, very lightly with white.

Place roof on schoolhouse again and attach with 1″ corner braces, one at each corner as shown.

Doors

Cut and assemble as shown in DOUBLE DOORS drawing. Hinges are placed so that the doors open out. Paint white. Install in doorway.

Sign

Cut and assemble as shown in SCHOOLHOUSE SIGN drawing. After painting, coat with one layer of polyurethane. Attach above doorway.

Belfry

Cut plywood for belfry (PLYWOOD PATTERNS FOR BELFRY). Attach trim (beveled at top and bottom as needed) as shown in BELFRY ASSEMBLY but do not assemble yet with the corner braces. Install 3″ wide siding strips. Drill holes for Bell Assembly. Paint interior side of panels and trim white. Paint siding red.

Construct BELL ASSEMBLY and PULL LEVER as shown. Do not attach the circles or pull lever to the bell assembly. Paint all but the circles and pull lever black. Paint those red. Put the dowels through the holes on the side panels and finish putting together the bell assembly and the belfry. Stick the end of a 4′ string or cord through the hole in the pull lever and tie a knot on the upper side.

Paint belfry roof to match schoolhouse roof. The weight of the belfry will keep it in position on the roof, but if you prefer you can attach it with screws from inside the schoolhouse.

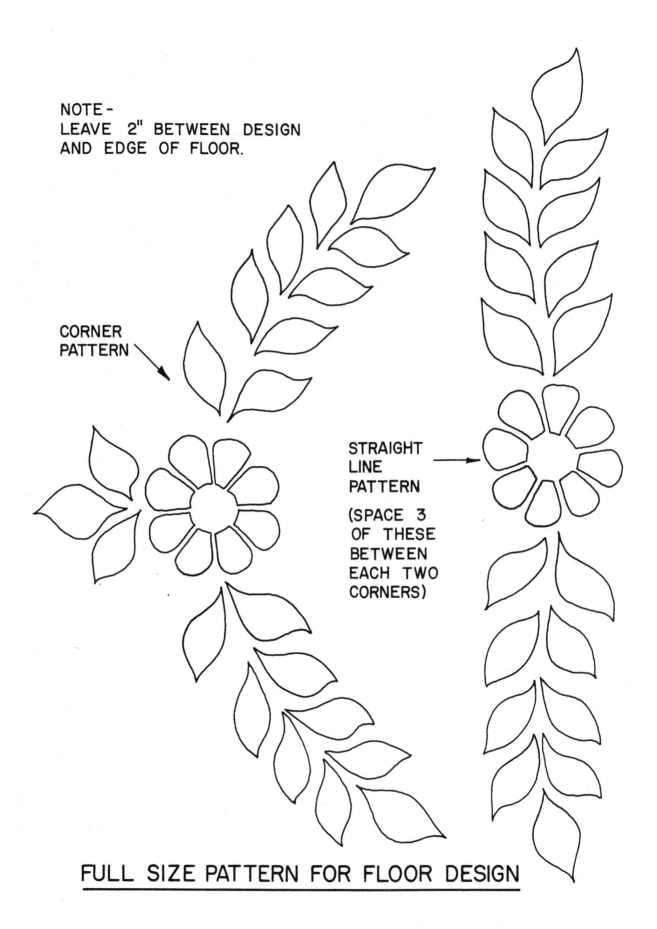

NOTE -
LEAVE 2" BETWEEN DESIGN
AND EDGE OF FLOOR.

CORNER
PATTERN

STRAIGHT
LINE
PATTERN

(SPACE 3
OF THESE
BETWEEN
EACH TWO
CORNERS)

FULL SIZE PATTERN FOR FLOOR DESIGN

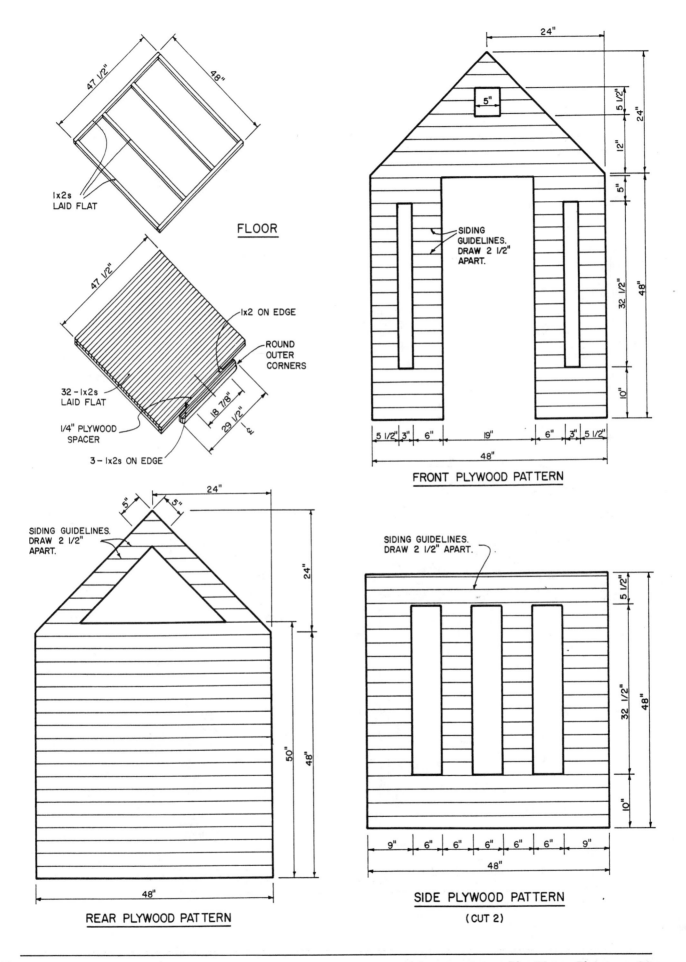

FLOOR

1x2s
LAID FLAT

47 1/2"

48"

47 1/2"

1x2 ON EDGE

ROUND
OUTER
CORNERS

32 – 1x2s
LAID FLAT

1/4" PLYWOOD
SPACER

3 – 1x2s ON EDGE

18 7/8"

29 1/2"

FRONT PLYWOOD PATTERN

24"

5"

5 1/2"

24"

12"

5"

SIDING
GUIDELINES.
DRAW 2 1/2"
APART.

32 1/2"

48"

10"

5 1/2" 3" 6"   19"   6" 3" 5 1/2"

48"

REAR PLYWOOD PATTERN

SIDING GUIDELINES.
DRAW 2 1/2"
APART.

5"   5"   24"

24"

50"

48"

48"

SIDE PLYWOOD PATTERN

(CUT 2)

SIDING GUIDELINES.
DRAW 2 1/2" APART.

5 1/2"

32 1/2"

48"

10"

9"   6"   6"   6"   6"   6"   9"

48"

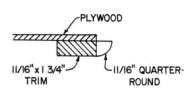

ATTACH PEAK SUPPORT
TO INTERIOR SIDE

6 EQUALLY SPACED SLATS
MADE FROM 1/4" PLYWOOD,
1/2" WIDE. MAKE 1/4"
DEEP NOTCHES IN SIDE
TRIM TO ACCOMMODATE
SLATS.

3/4" x 3/4"
TRIM

11/16" x 1 3/4"
TRIM

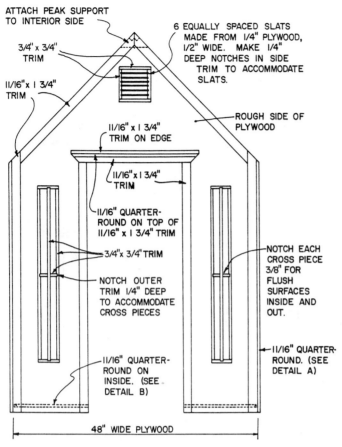

11/16" x 1 3/4"
TRIM ON EDGE

11/16" x 1 3/4"
TRIM

ROUGH SIDE OF
PLYWOOD

11/16" QUARTER-
ROUND ON TOP OF
11/16" x 1 3/4" TRIM

3/4" x 3/4" TRIM

NOTCH OUTER
TRIM 1/4" DEEP
TO ACCOMMODATE
CROSS PIECES

NOTCH EACH
CROSS PIECE
3/8" FOR
FLUSH
SURFACES
INSIDE AND
OUT.

11/16" QUARTER-
ROUND ON INSIDE. (SEE
DETAIL B)

11/16" QUARTER-
ROUND. (SEE
DETAIL A)

48" WIDE PLYWOOD

FRONT TRIM

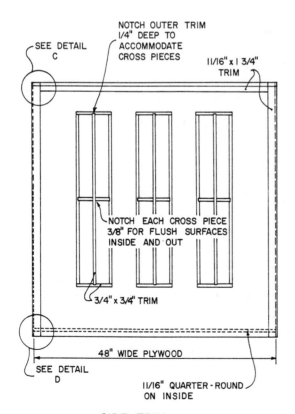

NOTCH OUTER TRIM
1/4" DEEP TO
ACCOMMODATE
CROSS PIECES

11/16" x 1 3/4"
TRIM

SEE DETAIL
C

NOTCH EACH CROSS PIECE
3/8" FOR FLUSH SURFACES
INSIDE AND OUT

3/4" x 3/4" TRIM

SEE DETAIL
D

48" WIDE PLYWOOD

11/16" QUARTER-ROUND
ON INSIDE

SIDE TRIM

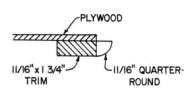

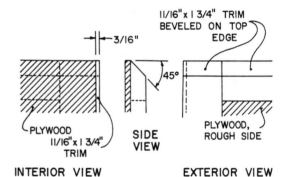

PLYWOOD

11/16" x 1 3/4"
TRIM

11/16" QUARTER-
ROUND

DETAIL A
CROSS-SECTION

BEVEL OUTER
ENDS OF
QUARTER ROUND
AT 45° ANGLE

QUARTER ROUND

PLYWOOD, SMOOTH
SIDE

3/16"

48"

3/16"

BOTTOM EDGE OF FRONT

DETAIL B
INTERIOR VIEW

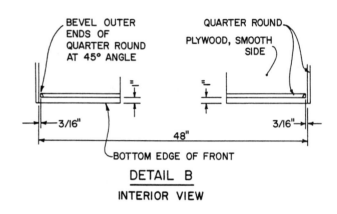

3/16"

11/16" x 1 3/4" TRIM
BEVELED ON TOP
EDGE

PLYWOOD
11/16" x 1 3/4"
TRIM

SIDE
VIEW

45°

PLYWOOD,
ROUGH SIDE

INTERIOR VIEW

EXTERIOR VIEW

DETAIL C

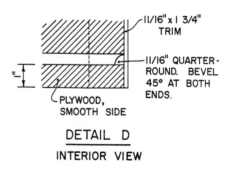

11/16" x 1 3/4"
TRIM

11/16" QUARTER-
ROUND. BEVEL
45° AT BOTH
ENDS.

PLYWOOD,
SMOOTH SIDE

DETAIL D
INTERIOR VIEW

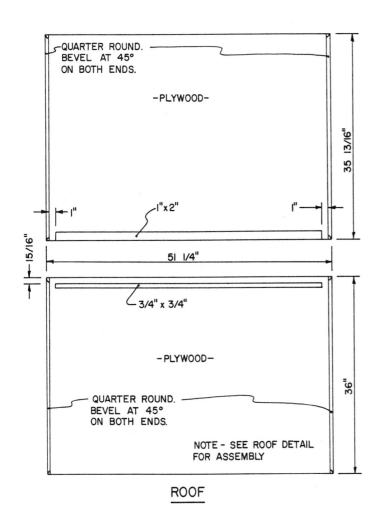

QUARTER ROUND.
BEVEL AT 45°
ON BOTH ENDS.

-PLYWOOD-

35 13/16"

1"

1"x2"

1"

51 1/4"

15/16"

3/4" x 3/4"

-PLYWOOD-

36"

QUARTER ROUND.
BEVEL AT 45°
ON BOTH ENDS.

NOTE - SEE ROOF DETAIL
FOR ASSEMBLY

ROOF

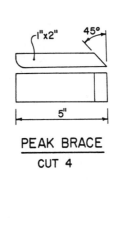

1"x2"

45°

5"

PEAK BRACE

CUT 4

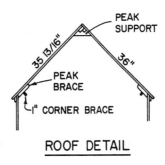

PEAK
SUPPORT

35 13/16"

36"

PEAK
BRACE

1" CORNER BRACE

ROOF DETAIL

CUT TWO FROM A SCRAP OF
1" THICK WOOD (OR GLUE
TOGETHER PIECES OF PLYWOOD
TO OBTAIN 1" THICKNESS).

FULL SIZE PATTERN FOR PEAK SUPPORT

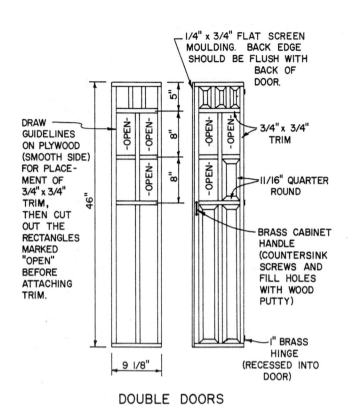

1/4" x 3/4" FLAT SCREEN MOULDING. BACK EDGE SHOULD BE FLUSH WITH BACK OF DOOR.

DRAW GUIDELINES ON PLYWOOD (SMOOTH SIDE) FOR PLACEMENT OF 3/4" x 3/4" TRIM, THEN CUT OUT THE RECTANGLES MARKED "OPEN" BEFORE ATTACHING TRIM.

3/4" x 3/4" TRIM

11/16" QUARTER ROUND

BRASS CABINET HANDLE (COUNTERSINK SCREWS AND FILL HOLES WITH WOOD PUTTY)

1" BRASS HINGE (RECESSED INTO DOOR)

DOUBLE DOORS

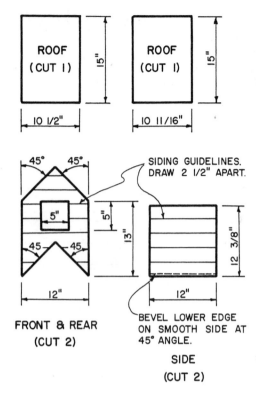

ROOF (CUT 1)   15"   10 1/2"

ROOF (CUT 1)   15"   10 11/16"

SIDING GUIDELINES. DRAW 2 1/2" APART.

45° 45°   5"   13"   45 45   12"

FRONT & REAR (CUT 2)

12 3/8"   12"

BEVEL LOWER EDGE ON SMOOTH SIDE AT 45° ANGLE.

SIDE (CUT 2)

PLYWOOD PATTERNS FOR BELFRY

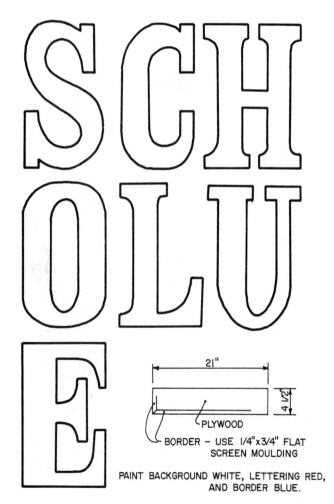

SCH OLU E

21"   4 1/2"

PLYWOOD

BORDER - USE 1/4" x 3/4" FLAT SCREEN MOULDING

PAINT BACKGROUND WHITE, LETTERING RED, AND BORDER BLUE.

SCHOOLHOUSE SIGN

3/4" x 3/4" TRIM

11/16" x 11/16" QUARTER ROUND

3/4" x 3/4" TRIM ON TOP EDGE AND AROUND WINDOW

PLYWOOD (BACK)

11/16" x 1 3/4" TRIM

3/4" x 3/4" TRIM

1 3/4" DIA. CIRCLE

1 3/4" DIA. CIRCLE

1x2

1/2" DIA. HOLE CENTERED ON SIDE AND 2" BELOW TOP OF PLYWOOD.

PULL LEVER

5" DIA. BELL

SMALL HOLE TO PUT PULL STRING THROUGH

1" CORNER BRACE (2 AT EACH CORNER)

BELFRY ASSEMBLY

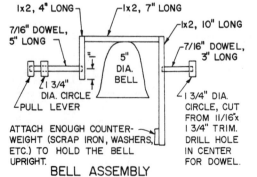

1x2, 4" LONG   1x2, 7" LONG

7/16" DOWEL, 5" LONG   1x2, 10" LONG

5" DIA. BELL

7/16" DOWEL, 3" LONG

1 3/4" DIA. CIRCLE PULL LEVER

1 3/4" DIA. CIRCLE, CUT FROM 11/16" x 1 3/4" TRIM. DRILL HOLE IN CENTER FOR DOWEL.

ATTACH ENOUGH COUNTER-WEIGHT (SCRAP IRON, WASHERS, ETC.) TO HOLD THE BELL UPRIGHT.

BELL ASSEMBLY

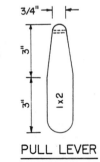

3/4"   3"   3"   1x2

PULL LEVER

FAIRY PRINCESS PLAY HOUSE

Designed by Kathy Smith Anthenat

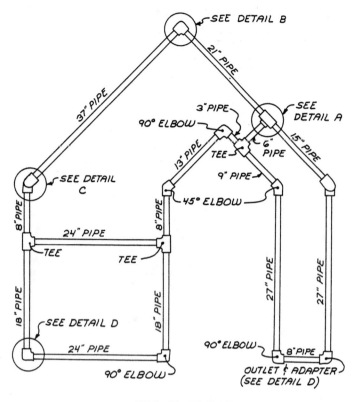

SEE DETAIL B

21" PIPE

37" PIPE

3" PIPE

90° ELBOW

SEE DETAIL A

13" PIPE

TEE

6" PIPE

15" PIPE

SEE DETAIL C

9" PIPE

45° ELBOW

8" PIPE

8" PIPE

24" PIPE

TEE

TEE

18" PIPE

18" PIPE

27" PIPE

27" PIPE

SEE DETAIL D

24" PIPE

90° ELBOW

8" PIPE

90° ELBOW

OUTLET & ADAPTER (SEE DETAIL D)

FRONT FRAME

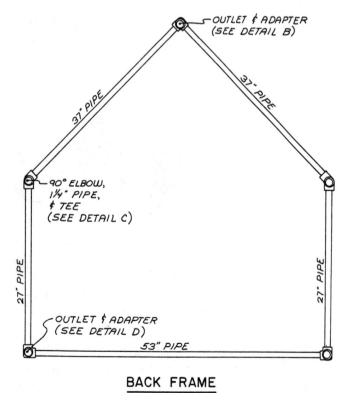

OUTLET & ADAPTER (SEE DETAIL B)

37" PIPE

37" PIPE

90° ELBOW, 1¼" PIPE, & TEE (SEE DETAIL C)

27" PIPE

27" PIPE

OUTLET & ADAPTER (SEE DETAIL D)

53" PIPE

BACK FRAME

Any little girl would feel like a fairy princess in this adorable play house. The shimmery baroque satin fabric which covers the PVC pipe frame is so delightful to touch and is also machine washable. What a wonderful place for afternoons of fantasy fun! The Fairy Princess Play House stands 56″ tall, 56″ wide, and 27″ deep—narrow enough to fit through most household doorways when assembled. The supplies to construct the one shown in the photograph totaled $27 for the PVC pipe frame and $54 for the fabric covering. Other fabrics could be substituted. Often you can buy flat sheets for the fabric for less money than buying fabric by the yard. Or you could use pieces of fabric left over from other projects to construct a "house-of-many-colors."

BILL OF MATERIALS

5 — 10′ lengths ¾″ PVC pipe
¾″ PVC pipe fittings:
6 — outlets
6 — adapters
8 — tees
2 — 45 degree elbows
8 — 90 degree elbows
1 — 8 oz. can PVC pipe cleaner
1 — 4 oz. can PVC pipe cement
45″ wide baroque satin fabric:
white — 2 yards
pink — 5 yards
dusty rose — 4 yards
lavender — 9 yards
thread
hook-and-loop tape — 6 tabs
(additional tabs are optional; see TIE DETAIL)

INSTRUCTIONS

PVC Pipe Frame

1 Cut pipe to required lengths as shown in FRONT FRAME and BACK FRAME diagrams. The following lengths of pipe are required to connect the front frame to the back frame:
two — @ 16½″
two — @ 19″
one — @ 21″

2 Use PVC pipe cleaner to remove any printing on the pieces. Be sure to work in a well-ventilated area. Remove any burrs on cut ends with coarse sandpaper.

3 Pre-assemble play house frame *WITHOUT CEMENT* as illustrated in DETAILS A, B, C, and D to be sure all pieces have been cut correctly. Reassemble play house, using directions on back of can to permanently bond the parts together with PVC pipe cement. Again, be sure to work in a well-ventilated area.

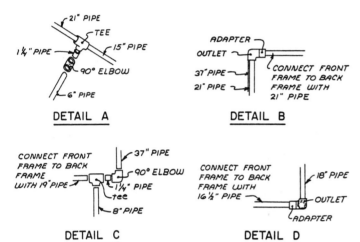

DETAIL A

DETAIL B

DETAIL C

DETAIL D

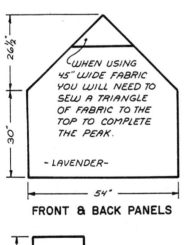

FRONT & BACK PANELS

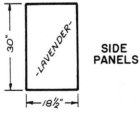

SIDE PANELS

FABRIC PATTERNS

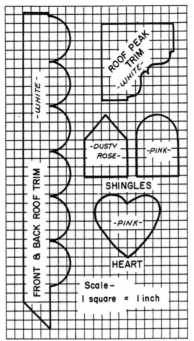

Fabric Walls

Note: The fabric covering is actually three pieces: the front and sides panel, the back panel, and the roof.

1 Cut a front panel, a back panel, and two side panels from lavender satin, using dimensions on FABRIC PATTERNS diagram. Press under 1″ along bottom edge of all four pieces. Press under 1″ again for a triple thickness 1″ wide hem. Stitch ¼″ from upper edge. The right side of this fabric will be the interior wall of the play house.

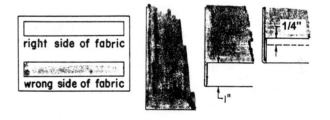

right side of fabric

wrong side of fabric

2 On the "wrong" side of the fabric use a pencil and ruler to draw horizontal guidelines 3″ apart, beginning 3″ from bottom edge of hem and continuing to the top of each of the four pieces.

3 Cut lavender siding strips 4″ wide. You will need ten strips for each panel—54″ long for the front and back panels and 18½″ long for the side panels.

Place the right side of a siding strip even with top edge of hem. Sew ¼" from top edge (see a.). Fold the siding strip up and place edge even with first guideline. Temporarily pin or baste in place. Place next siding strip right side down on top of first strip and sew ¼" from edge (see b.). Continue on up (see c.) until you have ten rows on each panel. The top row on the side panels will not be full height. Trim excess and baste top edge. This siding is the exterior side of the play house walls.

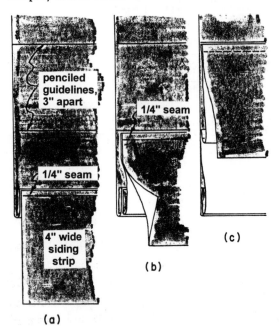

4 Cut a piece of dusty rose satin 80″ × 27¼″. Set aside to use later for the roof. Cut two siding strips of dusty rose—each 4½″ by 54″. Press under ½″ along one long edge on each strip; this will be the top edge. Sew to front and back panels with method described in Step 3, resulting in one row of dusty rose siding above ten rows of lavender siding. Place top pressed edge of dusty rose strip even with next higher guideline. Topstitch ¼″ from edge.

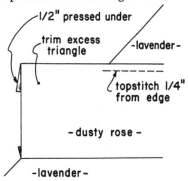

Shingles

1 Cut pink rounded shingles and dusty rose pointed shingles using patterns in FABRIC PATTERNS (page 29). Enlarge using 1 square = 1 inch scale. The play house pictured used forty-four pink shingles and eight dusty rose shingles. The number required may vary slightly according to the placement of the beginning row of shingles. Each finished shingle requires a pair of pieces. Sew together, leaving the 5″ straight side open. Turn right side out. Press.

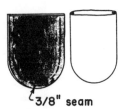

2 To sew shingles on front and back panels, place shingles above guideline, starting at the top edge of the dusty rose siding and lining up the straight edge of the shingle with the guideline. Stitch ¼″ from edge. Fold shingle down. Topstitch ½″ from edge. It is best to position and pin an entire row before sewing. Use pink shingles for the first two rows, dusty rose for the third row, and pink for the remaining rows. Space the shingles so that the center bottom of one shingle is located at the junction of the two shingles below it. Trim excess along the edges to maintain the angle of the peak.

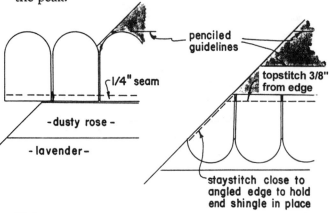

Trim

1 Cut four 6″x30″ strips of lavender satin. Press in a triple hem on one end of each strip (see Step 1). Do not sew hem. Place one of the strips along the side edge of the front panel on the outside, and one strip along this edge on the inside (see a.). Sew ⅜″ from edge. Sew outside strip to a side panel (see b.). Fold under ⅜″ along the edge of the other strip and slipstitch to interior side of side panel (see c.). Slipstitch bottom edge closed. Repeat with other side panel.

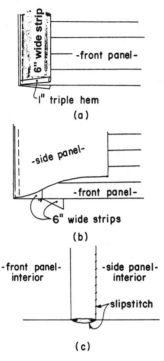

2 Cut two 7″ × 30″ strips of lavender. Press in a triple hem (see Step 1) on one end of each strip. Do not sew hem. Place along rear edge of side, right side of strip against exterior side of panel (see a.), and stitch ⅜″ from edge. Press under ⅜″ of remaining edge of strip and slipstitch to interior side of side panel (see b.).

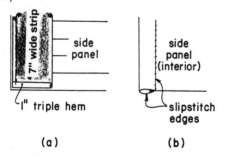

3 Cut two more 7″ × 30″ strips of lavender, piecing together fabric if necessary to obtain the needed size. Repeat Step 2 to sew these to the sides of the back panel.

4 Cut 4″ wide pink strips, piecing them together for the length required to go around the top of the front and side panels. Press under ½″ along a side, and ½″ on each end. Place right side of strip against exterior side of panel and sew, using a ½″ seam. Fold the strip over the top edge of the panel, fold under ½″, and slipstitch to interior side of panel. Repeat with back panel.

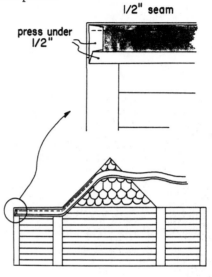

Ties

1 See TIE DETAIL for making ties to fasten panels to frame. Attach ties at indicated locations. Sew hooks of the hook-and-loop tape to interior edges of front and sides panel at indicated locations. Attach both panels to the PVC pipe frame, and mark the required locations for the loops of the hook-and-loop tape on the exterior side of the back panel as shown. Sew them on.

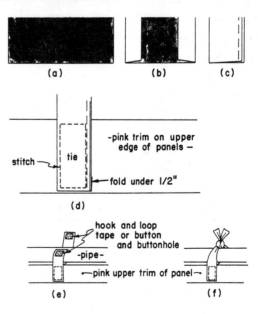

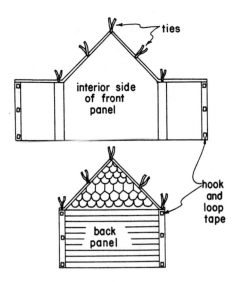

Tie Detail

Cut strips of fabric, 2¼″ wide, in a color to match the fabric at location of tie. Press under ⅜″ along each edge (see b.). Fold in half and stitch close to edge (see c.). Fold under ½″ on one end of two ties. Place in desired location on either side of pink trim on panel and stitch (see d.).

There are three options for fastening the ties: hook- and-loop tape (see e.), button and buttonhole, or tying them in a knot (see f.). Ties used for tying knots need to be longer than those using the other two methods. Buttons are not recommended because of the danger to small children if they become loose enough to pull off and swallow.

The ties at the doorway, window, and roof can be one piece — twice the length and sewn in the center to the seam on the panel of roof.

Door and Window

1 With both panels securely in place on the frame, use straight pins to mark the opening-side edge

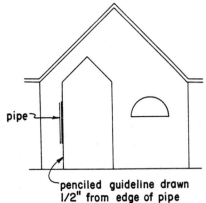

of the door frame pipe and the upper edge of the window bar pipe. Remove front panel from frame and lay flat on a table, interior side up. Using a straight edge, draw a door opening ½″ smaller than your straight pin outline. Draw a line ½″ above the window bar pins, and center a semi-circle window on this line (trace half of a pizza pan). Be sure that all shingles are lying flat—pin them if necessary—and cut out the doorway and window. Reinforce these edges by stitching ¼″ from edge.

2 Cut 2″ wide dusty rose bias strips, sewing together pieces for enough length to go around the window. Pin to edge of window on the exterior side. Stitch ½″ from edge. Turn to inside of window, fold under ½″, and slipstitch to interior side.

3 Cut 4″ wide strips for the doorway—three pink and four white. Measure the doorway for the required length and add an extra 2″ on the top and ½″ on the bottom. The unfinished bottom ends of the strips should end about 4″ from the floor. Fold the strips in half along the length, right sides together, and stitch ⅜″ from edge. Turn right side out. Press with the seam centered in the back.

4 Cut and sew together enough 2″ wide dusty rose bias strips to go around the doorway twice. Pin a bias strip to the interior side of the door, right side down (see a.). Stitch ½″ from the edge. Turn strip to exterior side of panel and pin in place (see b.). Pin doorway strips in place (see c.). Place another bias strip right side down on top of the first bias strip and the doorway strips (see c.). Stitch ½″ from edge. Turn outer bias strip out to lie flat against siding, right side up. Turn under ½″ and slipstitch to siding and shingles, or machine stitch very close to edge (see d.). Trim all doorway strips to same length. Tuck ½″ inside on the bottom ends of the strips and stitch ends closed.

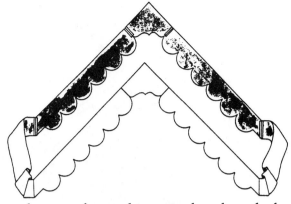

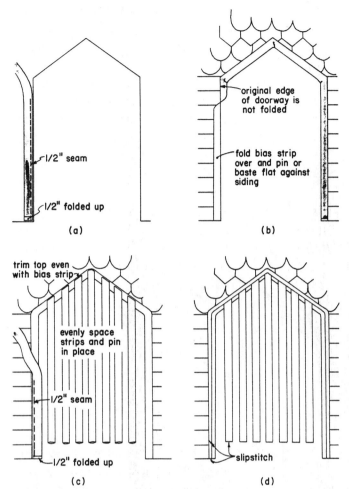

(a)

1/2" seam

1/2" folded up

(b)

original edge of doorway is not folded

fold bias strip over and pin or baste flat against siding

(c)

trim top even with bias strip

evenly space strips and pin in place

1/2" seam

1/2" folded up

(d)

slipstitch

5 Attach ties or fasteners at the locations shown. Fasten on frame.

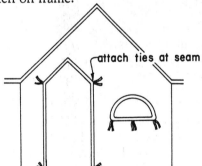

attach ties at seam

Roof

1 Enlarge pattern for ROOF PEAK TRIM and FRONT & BACK ROOF TRIM using FABRIC PATTERNS (page 29) and a 1 square = 1 inch scale. Cut four white roof peak trims and eight white front & back roof trims. Also cut four white 27½" × 4¼" rectangles for side roof trim. Sew pieces together to form two roof trim loops as shown. With right sides

together, sew the two loops together along the bottom edges (⅜" seam). Clip curves. Turn right side out. Press. Press under ⅜" along top edge of one of the loops.

2 Slightly round the corners of the dusty rose roof rectangle that you cut in Step 4. Fold the rectangle in half to find the center of each long side and pin unpressed point of roof peak to it, right sides together. Continue pinning the rest of the trim to the roof, easing around rounded corners. Stitch ⅜" from edge. Slipstitch edge which was pressed under to wrong side of roof.

3 Attach ties to each corner of the roof and to roof peaks—at the seam joining the dusty rose and white satin. Fasten to frame.

Heart

1 Enlarge HEART pattern using FABRIC PATTERNS (page 29) and a 1 square = 1 inch scale. Cut two from pink satin. Embroider or write name on one heart piece with fabric paint.

2 With right sides together, stitch hearts ⅜" from edge, leaving an opening along one side to turn. Turn right side out. Press. Stuff loosely. Slipstitch opening closed.

3 Fold a 7" piece of narrow green ribbon in half. Sew the two ends to the upper center of the stuffed heart. If desired, decorate that area with tiny ribbon roses (available at the craft or fabric store). Sew top of ribbon to play house. Do not attach heart to play house; let it hang free from the ribbon.

COMBINATION LOG CABIN PLAY HOUSE/ STORAGE SHED

Designed by Bruce A. Anthenat

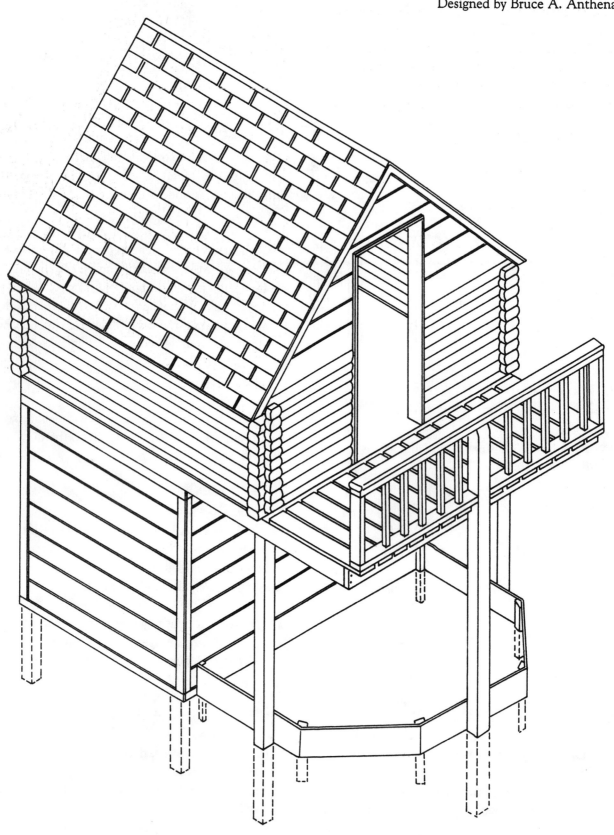

Let the kids help decide how to get up to and down from this play house, which uses landscape timbers to imitate a log cabin. Add a slide, ladder, rope, chain of tires, or fireman's pole to make it uniquely theirs. Store your lawn mower and garden supplies conveniently in the shed underneath. Or eliminate the shed and make a shaded sandbox of the entire underneath area. Perhaps you will decide to add a baby swing there now and frame in the shed next year.

BILL OF MATERIALS

6 — treated 4" × 4" × 8 posts
1 — treated 4" × 4" × 10' post
42 — 8' Landscape timbers
4 — treated 2" × 6" × 8'
2 — treated 2" × 6" × 10'
2 — treated 1" × 12" × 10'
1 — 8' Handrail
7 — 5/4" × 6" × 8' decking
12 — 2" × 4" × 8'
17 — 2" × 4" × 6'
7 — treated 2" × 4" × 8'
3¼ — 4' × 8' sheets ¼" CDX plywood
2 — 4' × 8' sheets ¾" treated plywood
6 — 4' × 8' sheets ⅝" v-groove siding
16 — 1" × 3" × 8' trim
1 square roof shingles
6 bags concrete mix
Concrete patio blocks
Door hinges
Deck screws

This version of the Combination Log Cabin Play House/Storage Shed includes stairs with a landing and railing, a bubble window in the roof, and a fireman's pole.

OPTIONAL STEPS WITH HANDRAIL

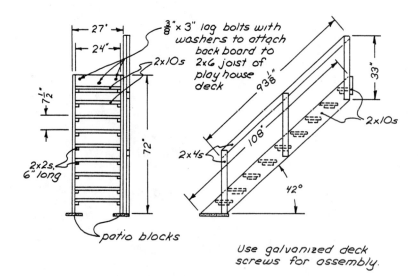

27"
24"
7 1/2"
72"
2x10s
3/8" x 3" lag bolts with washers to attach back board to 2x6 joist of play house deck
2x2s, 6" long
patio blocks
93 3/8"
108"
33"
2x10s
2x4s
42"

Use galvanized deck screws for assembly.

REQUIRED MATERIALS

treated 2x10s, 2 @ 10' long & 4 @ 6' long
treated 2x4s, 1 @ 10' long & 1 @ 8' long
treated 2x2s, 1 @ 10' long
3 - 3/8" x 3" lag bolts with washers
4 concrete patio blocks
galvanized deck screws.

OPTIONAL FIREMAN POLE

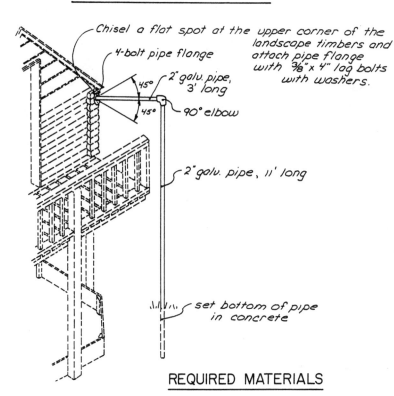

Chisel a flat spot at the upper corner of the landscape timbers and attach pipe flange with 3/8" x 4" lag bolts with washers.

4-bolt pipe flange
2" galu. pipe, 3' long
45°
45°
90° elbow
2" galu. pipe, 11' long
set bottom of pipe in concrete

REQUIRED MATERIALS

2" galvanized pipe, 3' long
2" galvanized pipe, 11' long
90° elbow for 2" pipe
Standard 4-bolt 2" pipe flange
concrete mix
4 - 3/8" x 4" lag bolts with washers

SUPPORT POSTS LAYOUT

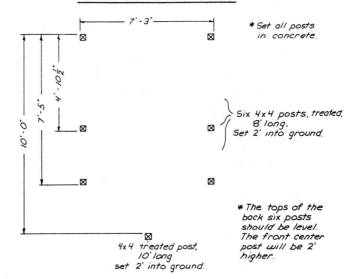

* Set all posts in concrete.

7'-3"

7'-5"

10'-0"

4'-10½"

Six 4x4 posts, treated, 8' long. Set 2' into ground.

* The tops of the back six posts should be level. The front center post will be 2' higher.

4x4 treated post, 10' long, set 2' into ground.

DETAIL OF NOTCHED TIMBER

Use circular saw with blade set at angle to make end cuts, then chisel out notch.

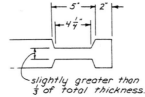

5"   2"

4¼"

slightly greater than ⅓ of total thickness.

* Front and back of play house require eleven landscape timbers each. Top timber and bottom timber should be notched on one side only.

Sides of play house require ten timbers each, plus a 2x4 spacer at top & bottom.

FLOOR JOISTS

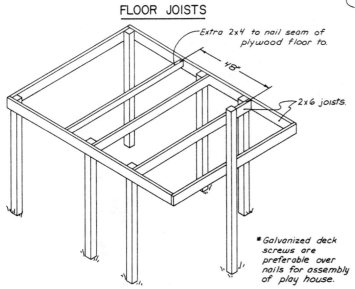

Extra 2x4 to nail seam of plywood floor to.

48"

2x6 joists.

* Galvanized deck screws are preferable over nails for assembly of play house.

ROOF DETAIL

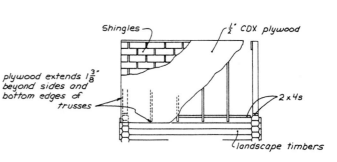

Shingles

½" CDX plywood

plywood extends 1⅜" beyond sides and bottom edges of trusses

2x4s

landscape timbers

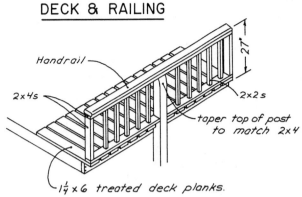

DECK & RAILING

Handrail

2x4s

2x2s

27"

taper top of post
to match 2x4

1¼ x 6 treated deck planks.

SANDBOX

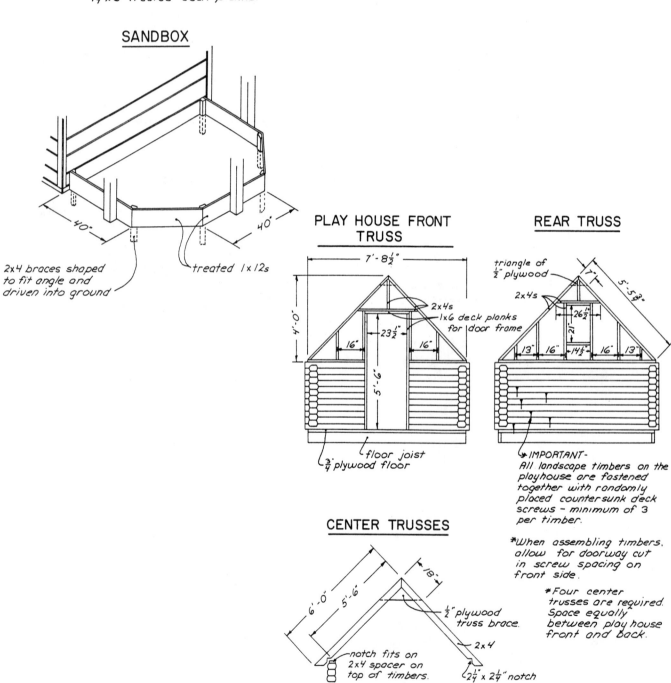

40'

40'

2x4 braces shaped
to fit angle and
driven into ground

treated 1x12s

PLAY HOUSE FRONT TRUSS

7'-8½"

4'-0"

2x4s
1x6 deck planks
for door frame

23½"

16"

16"

5'-6"

floor joist

¾" plywood floor

REAR TRUSS

triangle of
½" plywood

7'

5'-5¾"

2x4s

26½"

21"

13"

16"

14½"

16"

13"

*IMPORTANT-
All landscape timbers on the
playhouse are fastened
together with randomly
placed countersunk deck
screws - minimum of 3
per timber.

*When assembling timbers,
allow for doorway cut
in screw spacing on
front side.

*Four center
trusses are required.
Space equally
between play house
front and back.

CENTER TRUSSES

18"

6'-0"

5'-6"

½" plywood
truss brace.

2x4

notch fits on
2x4 spacer on
top of timbers.

2¼ x 2¼" notch

STORAGE SHED STUD DETAIL

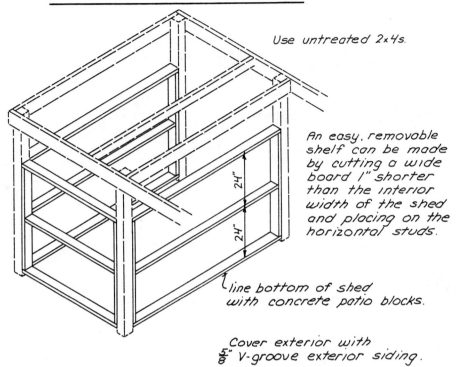

Use untreated 2x4s.

An easy, removable shelf can be made by cutting a wide board 1" shorter than the interior width of the shed and placing on the horizontal studs.

24"

24"

line bottom of shed with concrete patio blocks.

Cover exterior with $\frac{5}{8}$" V-groove exterior siding.

SHED DOOR

(can be constructed on either end of shed)

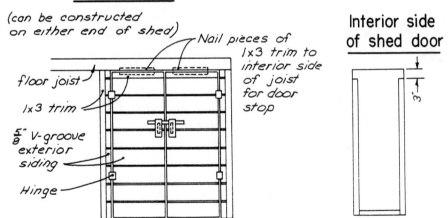

Nail pieces of 1x3 trim to interior side of joist for door stop

floor joist

1x3 trim

$\frac{5}{8}$" V-groove exterior siding

Hinge

Interior side of shed door

3"

COLONIAL DOLLHOUSE/PLAY HOUSE

Designed by Ken Manda Builders

It is the details that make this beautiful play house so eye-catching—an elegant oval window above the front door, windows with curtains and shutters, etc. In addition, the one shown was professionally landscaped for a Home and Garden Show at a mall, adding to the "real house" illusion.

The Colonial Dollhouse/Play House is 6' wide, 5' deep, and 6' high. Children enter through a 2' wide opening in the center of the back. Basic overall dimensions are given in the drawings, along with the locations of the door and window openings. The wood moulding required for trimming the windows and doors can be found at hobby and craft stores if not at a building supply store.

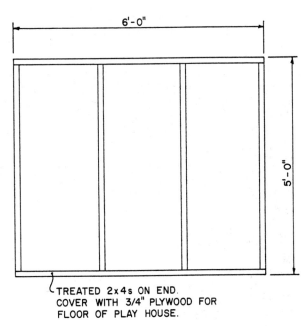

6'-0"

5'-0"

TREATED 2x4s ON END.
COVER WITH 3/4" PLYWOOD FOR
FLOOR OF PLAY HOUSE.

BASE

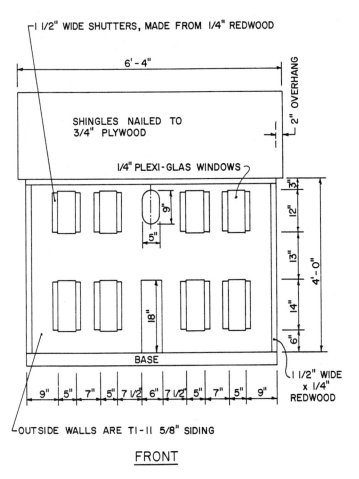

1 1/2" WIDE SHUTTERS, MADE FROM 1/4" REDWOOD

6'-4"

2" OVERHANG

SHINGLES NAILED TO
3/4" PLYWOOD

1/4" PLEXI-GLAS WINDOWS

9"

5"

3"
12"
13"
14"
6"

4'-0"

18"

BASE

9" 5" 7" 5" 7 1/2" 6" 7 1/2" 5" 7" 5" 9"

1 1/2" WIDE
x 1/4"
REDWOOD

OUTSIDE WALLS ARE TI-11 5/8" SIDING

FRONT

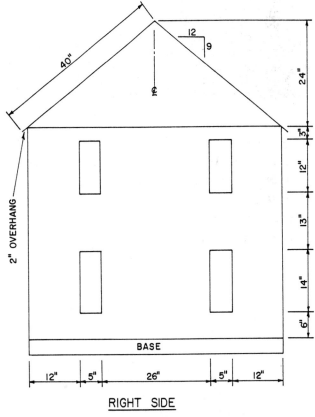

40"

12
9

24"

3"
12"
13"
14"
6"

2" OVERHANG

BASE

12" 5" 26" 5" 12"

RIGHT SIDE

1. 2x2 FRAME TO BE CONSTRUCTED FIRST.
2. 5/8" TI-11 SIDING INSTALLED ON 2x2 FRAME.
3. SHUTTER ALL WINDOWS SAME AS FRONT.

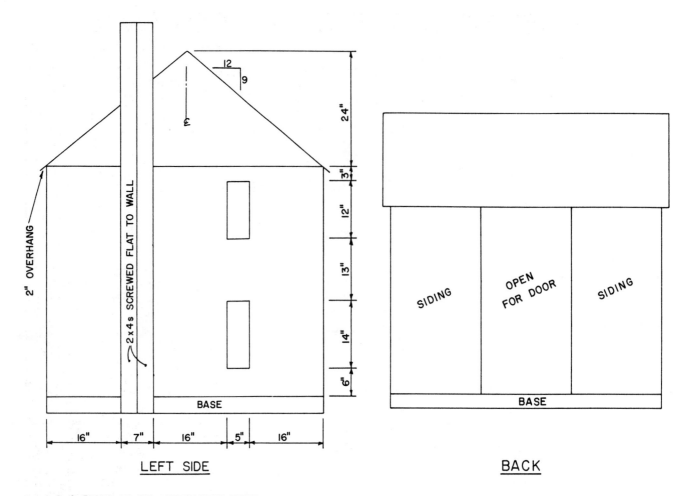

LEFT SIDE   BACK

1. 2x2 FRAME TO BE CONSTRUCTED FIRST.

2. 5/8" TI-11 SIDING INSTALLED ON 2x2 FRAME.

3. SHUTTER ALL WINDOWS SAME AS FRONT.

SUNSHINE AND FLOWERS COTTAGE

Designed by Kathy Smith Anthenat

Used cardboard boxes (free from a furniture store) were transformed into this charming indoor play house. The base is made from a 37″ × 32″ box, 50″ tall and open at both ends to make it collapsible to fit through doorways. Large pieces of flat cardboard (from a mattress shipping box) were fashioned into a removable roof. You will need to modify the instructions below to accommodate the size of the box you are able to obtain.

INSTRUCTIONS

Cutting the Base

With a craft knife, cut a lattice-style window and a doorway from a 37″ wide side of the box as shown in FRONT drawing. Cut a lattice-style window and an open window on each 32″ wide side as shown in SIDES drawing. The two window heights allow a small child to look out from a sitting or standing position. The bottom window is open because little ones find tossing toys and stuffed animals in and out of a window wonderfully fun!

No openings are cut in the back of the play house. Cut off the small triangles as shown at the top of the front and back. Score (cut through the outside layer of the corrugated cardboard only) a line 4″ from the top on the sides; fold inside and glue flat to the side to provide extra strength. Use whatever adhesive you have available. One inexpensive and easy to use option is paneling adhesive. You can attach extra cardboard on the inside anywhere you need extra

strength to keep the play house from bending, such as directly above the peak of the doorway.

Painting the Base

Paint the exterior of the box white—one coat. With a pencil, draw a 1″ wide window frame around each of the five windows. Put another coat of white paint on the window frames. Paint the rest of the exterior a soft yellow. With a broad-tip black marker outline the inner and outer edges of the window frame. Draw a line indicating corner trim 1″ from each corner. Draw horizontal lines 4″ apart to indicate siding.

Door

Cut a piece of cardboard for the door 14¾″ × 26″. Cut the three pieces of door trim as shown in DOOR TRIM drawing. Glue trim to door. Paint the trim yellow and the recessed areas white. Using duct tape for hinges, attach the door to the door opening. The bottom of the door should be about 2″ above the floor. The four hinges should be taped on the inside and outside for extra durability.

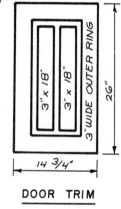

DOOR TRIM

Door Overhang

Cut the door overhang piece and two small triangles as shown. Score on fold lines. Fold. Glue the two triangles to the inside of the folded overhang in the center to hold it in an inverted V shape. Paint the

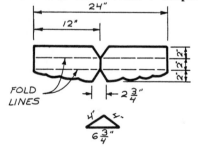

inside white and the outside yellow. Glue the overhang to the play house above the door opening.

Roof

Cut a flat piece of cardboard 40" × 50". Find the center of the 50" and score a line. Bend to make a gable roof with each side 40" × 25".

Cut two triangular peak pieces as shown. Score the fold lines. Fold. Glue each piece 3⅜" in from each end of the roof, with the folded flaps pointing inward.

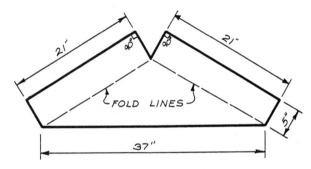

Paint the roof and peaks white. Place on top of the play house with the peaks outside the front and back walls.

Flowers

With a 1" foam brush and green paint, paint ivy leaves around the lattice-style windows. Paint flower stems of varying heights around the bottom of the play house. Add a few long slender leaves. Paint shorter grass around the bottom.

Make the paper flowers from white, lavender, and pink crépe paper (available in craft stores). Exact measurements aren't necessary but you will need four pieces of crépe paper, approximately 6" × 9", for each flower. The grain should run parallel to the 6" sides. Lay the pieces one on top of the other and fold up accordion-style, beginning at a 6" edge. The folds should be about ½" wide. Tie the center with string. Gently pull up the top sheet of crépe paper on one side of the string, making it perpendicular with the rest of the folds. Pull up the top sheet on the other side of the string. Repeat, alternating sides, until you have all of the sheet halves pulled up and fluffed out to make a flower.

Glue the flowers below the lattice-style windows and on each flower stem.

Details

You might want to add a cardboard mailbox beside the door with your child's name printed on it. Encourage your son or daughter to decorate the interior of the play house with his or her own artwork which has been framed with construction paper or leftover cardboard.

CARDBOARD CASTLE

Designed by Kathy Smith Anthenat

What a great way to use up leftovers: a leftover box from moving, leftover white ceiling paint, and leftover beige house paint. This disposable castle is a sure hit with preschoolers.

INSTRUCTIONS

1 If both ends of the box have flaps, cut off the flaps on one end and make this the bottom of the castle. The top flaps can either be cut off, or — if you want to make the castle higher — use masking tape to hold them together in an upright position. Bend the sides every few inches to turn the rectangular shape into a circular shape.

2 Use a pizza pan to draw a semi-circle for the top of the doorway, and a salad plate for the window. Cut them out with a craft knife or razor blade. Cut 8" × 5" notches in the top. Paint white. Note: Paint, besides being decorative, also seems to take care of the problem of the sharp cut edges. It dulls the edges just enough to prevent most paper cuts to little fingers.

3 Cut a piece of thin cardboard about 2" × 5". Round the edges and use it as a pattern to draw the bricks around the doorway and window. Paint the bricks beige and outline them with a broad-tip black marker.

4 Optional finishing touches:
    Use brightly colored fabric to make banners to wave above the castle.
    Paint your family surname or coat of arms above the door.

OFFICE SKYSCRAPER

Designed by Kathy Smith Anthenat

This box once contained a kitchen range but is now ready for hours of fun as a colorable play house. Children can use crayons and markers to add faces, hair, and clothes to the people standing at the base of the building and in the windows.

INSTRUCTIONS

1 The bottom of this open top box was held in place with a tight metal band. Remove the band and replace it with a more loosely fitting band of duct tape so that the lid can be taken on and off. This will make the box collapsible to fit through doorways. The lid is the flat roof of the skyscraper.

2 Cut out a doorway appropriately sized for your child on one side of the box.

3 Paint the box and lid white; at least two coats will probably be necessary to cover all the printing on the box. Do not use glossy paint; it is too hard to use crayons on.

4 With a broad-tip black marker draw the rows of 3″ × 4″ office windows on all four sides of the box, beginning 9″ above the floor. Use a craft knife or razor blade to cut out some of the window rectangles for peep holes.

5 Use the FULL SIZE PATTERNS FOR PEOPLE and a black marker to draw people at the base

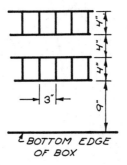

of the building and in the windows. Only three-quarters of the people in the windows will show. In some of the windows you might want to add simple flower pots with flowers, file cabinets, office signs, etc. If you are artistically inclined, a fun addition would be a giant gorilla climbing up the outside of the building!

FULL SIZE PATTERNS FOR PEOPLE

HEATHER'S HIDEAWAY

Designed by Jeff Short

This rustic log cabin uses landscape timbers for the walls, and has five windows and one door. The structure is approximately 8′ × 12′ and has a 4′ × 8′ porch — plenty of space for a play house, small workshop, office, or guest cottage.

NOTE -
SUPPORT JOINTS AND PROVIDE FOR
AIR FLOW UNDER HOUSE BY
PLACING PATIO BLOCKS UNDER
EACH JOINT.

STAGGER TIMBER
JOINT ON 12'
SIDES

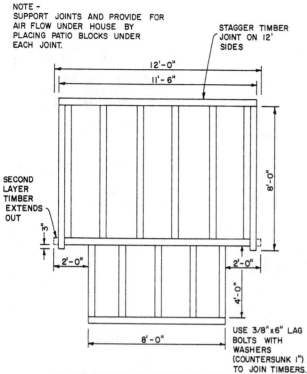

SECOND
LAYER
TIMBER
EXTENDS
OUT

USE 3/8"x6" LAG
BOLTS WITH
WASHERS
(COUNTERSUNK 1")
TO JOIN TIMBERS.

PLACEMENT OF FIRST LAYER
OF LANDSCAPE TIMBERS

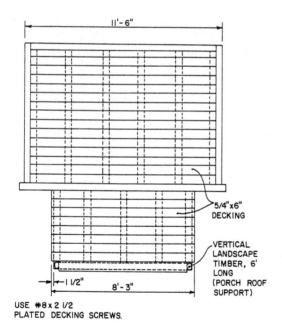

5/4"x6"
DECKING

VERTICAL
LANDSCAPE
TIMBER, 6'
LONG
(PORCH ROOF
SUPPORT)

USE #8 x 2 1/2
PLATED DECKING SCREWS.

SECOND LAYER OF LANDSCAPE TIMBERS
AND FLOORING

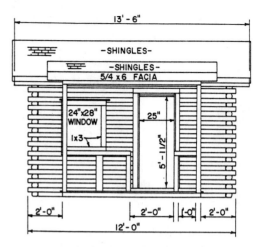

FRONT ELEVATION

NOTES-
a. TIMBERS ARE STACKED 26 LAYERS HIGH.
b. STAGGER JOINTS WHEN USING 1 1/2 TIMBERS FOR 12' LENGTHS.
c. USE STORM WINDOWS, ADJUSTING ROUGH OPENING TO FIT.
d. USE 1x3s FOR BASEBOARD INSIDE.
e. USE 1/2" CDX PLYWOOD FOR ROOF. FINISH WITH WOOD OR
   ASPHALT SHINGLES.

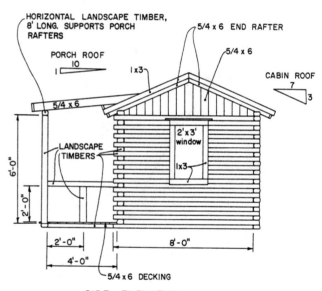

SIDE ELEVATION

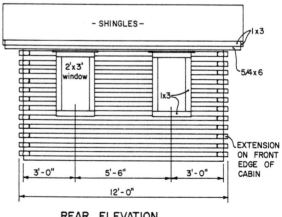

REAR ELEVATION

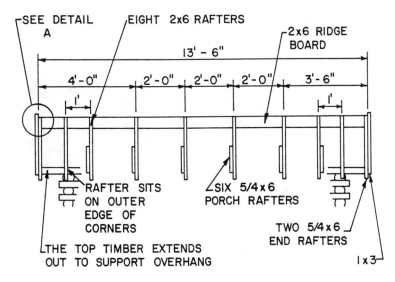

SEE DETAIL A

EIGHT 2x6 RAFTERS

2x6 RIDGE BOARD

13' - 6"

4'-0"   2'-0"   2'-0"   2'-0"   3'-6"

1'   1'

RAFTER SITS ON OUTER EDGE OF CORNERS

SIX 5/4 x 6 PORCH RAFTERS

TWO 5/4 x 6 END RAFTERS

1 x 3

THE TOP TIMBER EXTENDS OUT TO SUPPORT OVERHANG

FRONT VIEW OF RAFTER SPACING FOR

CABIN & PORCH

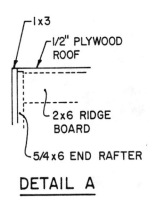

1 x 3

1/2" PLYWOOD ROOF

2x6 RIDGE BOARD

5/4 x 6 END RAFTER

DETAIL A

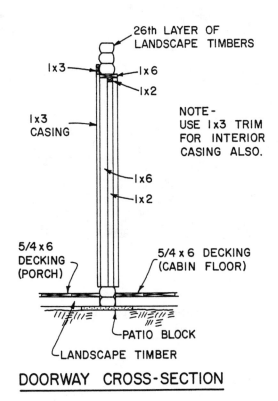

26th LAYER OF LANDSCAPE TIMBERS

1 x 3

1 x 6

1 x 2

1 x 3 CASING

NOTE - USE 1x3 TRIM FOR INTERIOR CASING ALSO.

1 x 6

1 x 2

5/4 x 6 DECKING (PORCH)

5/4 x 6 DECKING (CABIN FLOOR)

PATIO BLOCK

LANDSCAPE TIMBER

DOORWAY CROSS-SECTION

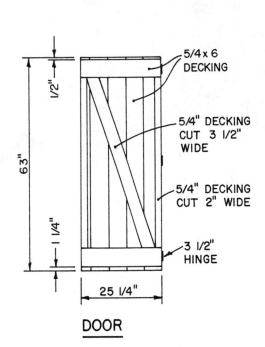

5/4 x 6 DECKING

1/2"

63"

1 1/4"

5/4" DECKING CUT 3 1/2" WIDE

5/4" DECKING CUT 2" WIDE

3 1/2" HINGE

25 1/4"

DOOR

CHESHIRE CAT PLAY HOUSE

Courtesy of the Southern Pine Marketing Council
Designer: Gary Panter

Courtesy of Southern Forest Products Association.

This whimsical play house will delight a whole neighborhood full of children, from the happy face with a big walk-through smile to the crooked doors and windows. It measures 8' × 17' and stands 12' tall. Through rain or shine, this wooden Cheshire cat keeps on smiling.

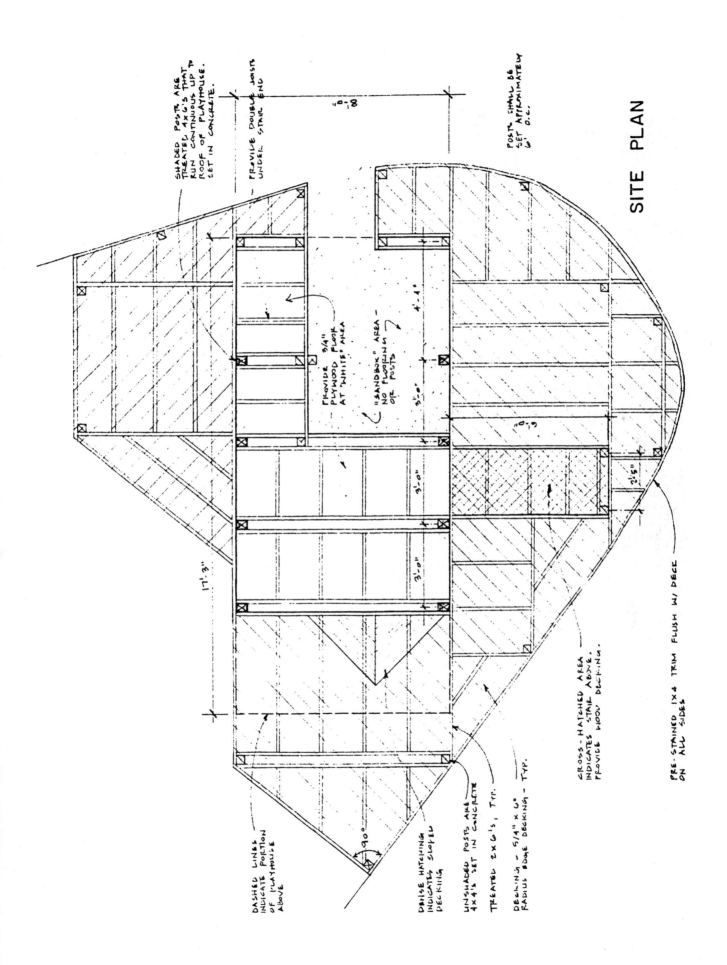

SITE PLAN

SHADED POSTS ARE TREATED 4x6'S THAT RUN CONTINUOUS UP TO ROOF OF PLAYHOUSE. SET IN CONCRETE.

PROVIDE DOUBLE JOISTS UNDER STAIR END

POSTS SHALL BE SET APPROXIMATELY 6' O.C.

8'-0"

PROVIDE 3/4" PLYWOOD FLOOR AT "WHITE" AREA

"SANDBOX" AREA — NO FLOORING OR POSTS

4'-4"

3'-0"

3'-0"

17'-3"

3'-0"

3'-0"

3'-0"

2'-5"

90°

DASHED LINES INDICATE PORTION OF PLAYHOUSE ABOVE

DENSE HATCHING INDICATES SLOPED DECKING

UNSHADED POSTS ARE 4x4'S SET IN CONCRETE

TREATED 2x6's, TYP.

DECKING — 5/4" x 6" RADIUS EDGE DECKING — TYP.

CROSS-HATCHED AREA INDICATES STAIR ABOVE. PROVIDE WOOD DECKING.

PRE-STAINED 1x4 TRIM FLUSH W/ DECK ON ALL SIDES

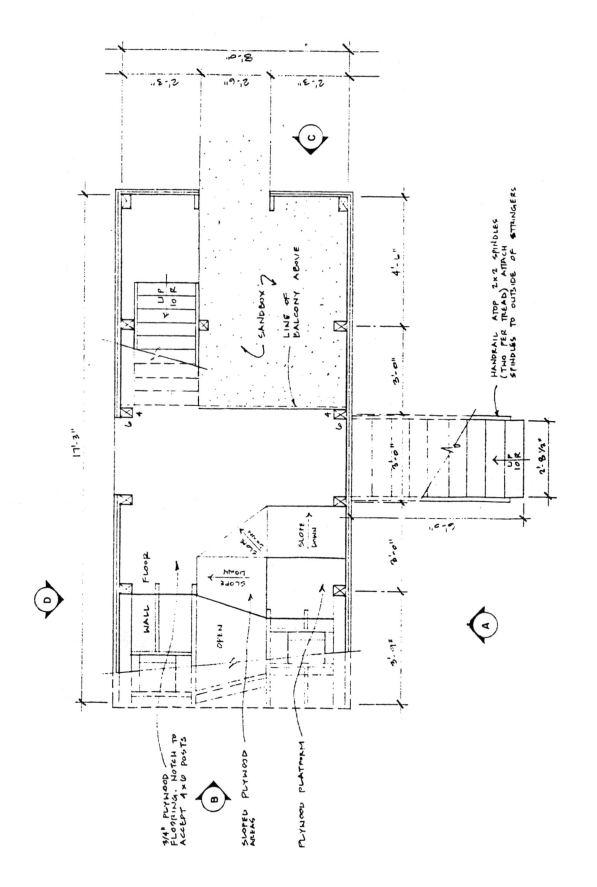

GROUND LEVEL PLAN

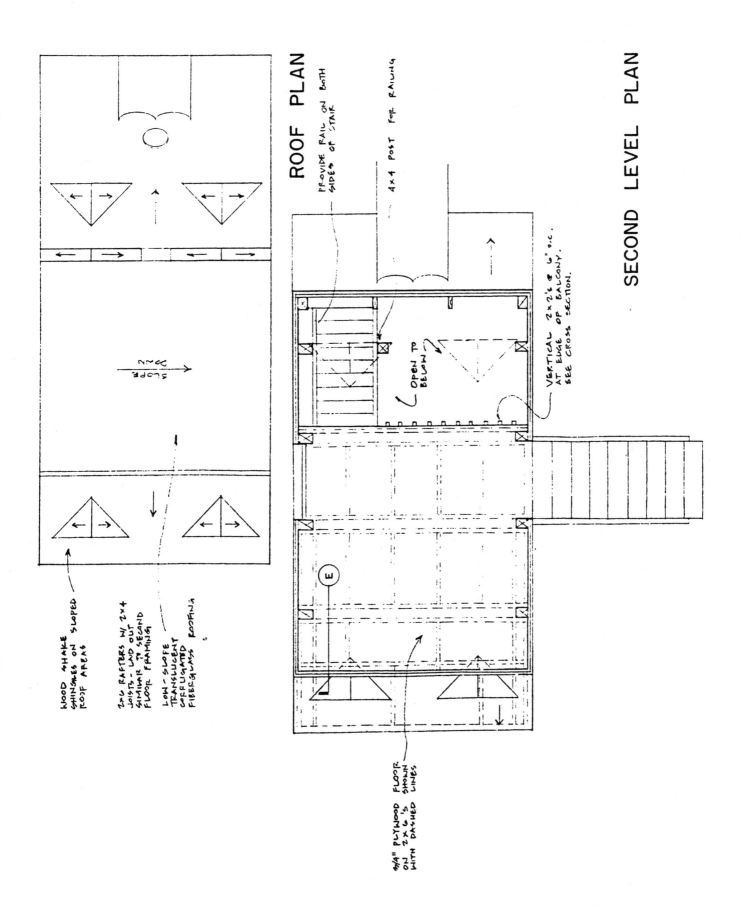

ROOF PLAN

SECOND LEVEL PLAN

PROVIDE RAIL ON BOTH SIDES OF STAIR

4x4 POST FOR RAILING

SLOPE DOWN

OPEN TO BELOW

VERTICAL 2x2's @ 6" o.c. AT EDGE OF BALCONY. SEE CROSS SECTION.

WOOD SHAKE SHINGLES ON SLOPED ROOF AREAS

2x6 RAFTERS w/ 2x4 JOISTS - LAID OUT SIMILAR TO SECOND FLOOR FRAMING

LOW-SLOPE TRANSLUCENT CORRUGATED FIBERGLASS ROOFING

5/4" PLYWOOD FLOOR ON 2x6's SHOWN WITH DASHED LINES

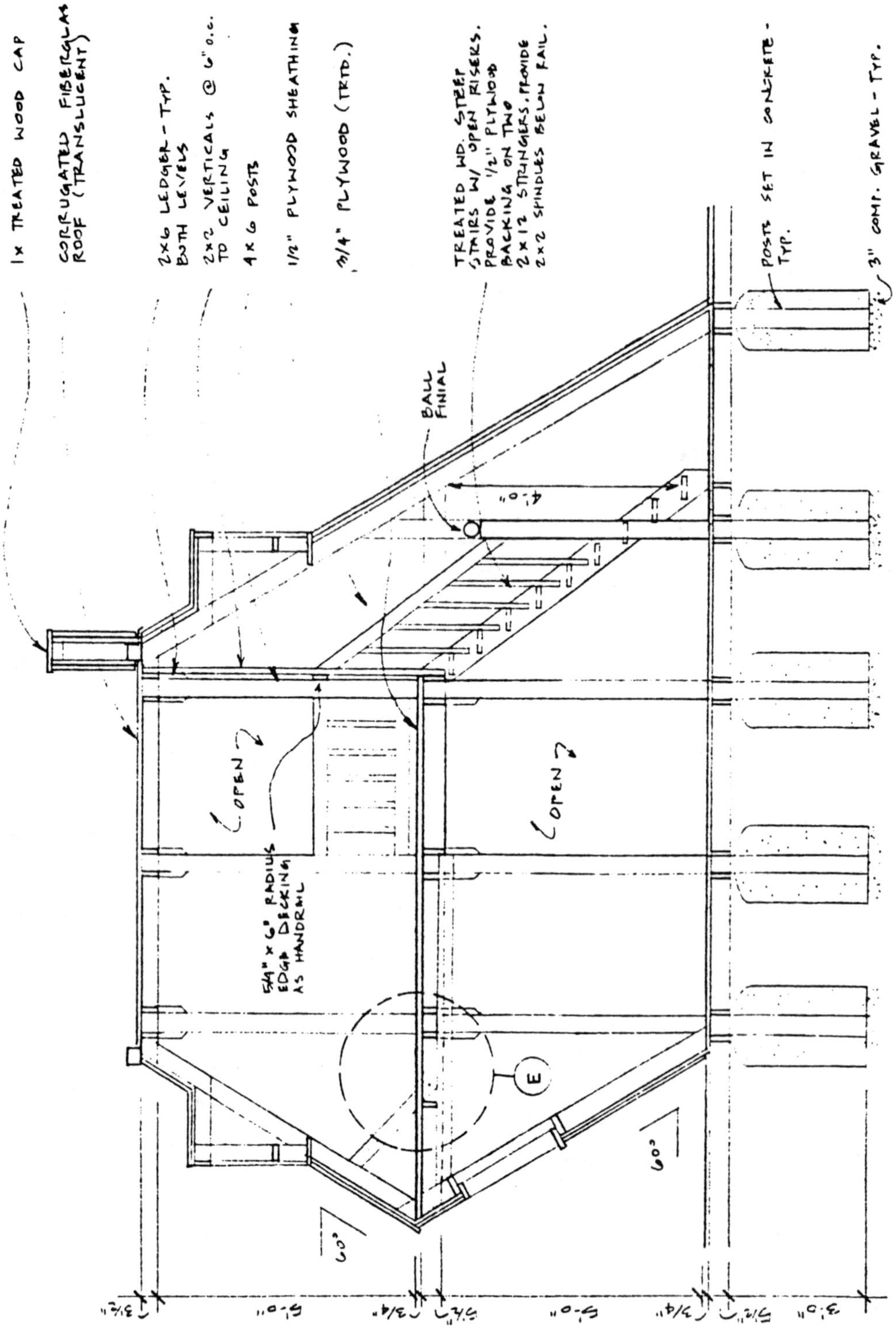

IX TREATED WOOD CAP

CORRUGATED FIBERGLASS ROOF (TRANSLUCENT)

2×6 LEDGER - TYP. BOTH LEVELS

2×2 VERTICALS @ 6" O.C. TO CEILING

4×6 POSTS

1/2" PLYWOOD SHEATHING

3/4" PLYWOOD (TRTD.)

TREATED WD. STEEP STAIRS W/ OPEN RISERS. PROVIDE 1/2" PLYWOOD BACKING ON TWO 2×12 STRINGERS. PROVIDE 2×2 SPINDLES BELOW RAIL.

POSTS SET IN CONCRETE - TYP.

3" COMP. GRAVEL - TYP.

BALL FINIAL

5/4" × 6" RADIUS EDGE DECKING AS HANDRAIL

OPEN

OPEN

E

4'-0"

6'-3"

3 1/2"

5'-0"

5/4" 3/4"

5/4" 3/4"

5'-0"

5/4" 3/4"

3 1/2"

3'-0"

CROSS SECTION

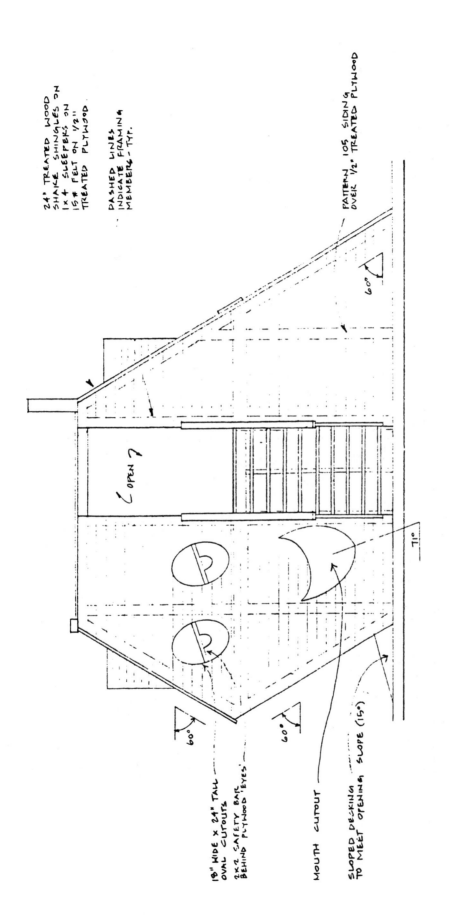

24" TREATED WOOD
SHAKE SHINGLES ON
1x4 SLEEPERS ON
15# FELT ON 1/2"
TREATED PLYWOOD

DASHED LINES
INDICATE FRAMING
MEMBERS - TYP.

PATTERN 105 SIDING
OVER 1/2" TREATED PLYWOOD

60°

OPEN

60°

71°

60°

18" WIDE x 24" TALL
OVAL CUTOUTS

2x2 SAFETY BAR
BEHIND PLYWOOD 'EYES'

MOUTH CUTOUT

SLOPED DECKING
TO MEET OPENING SLOPE (15°)

ELEVATION A

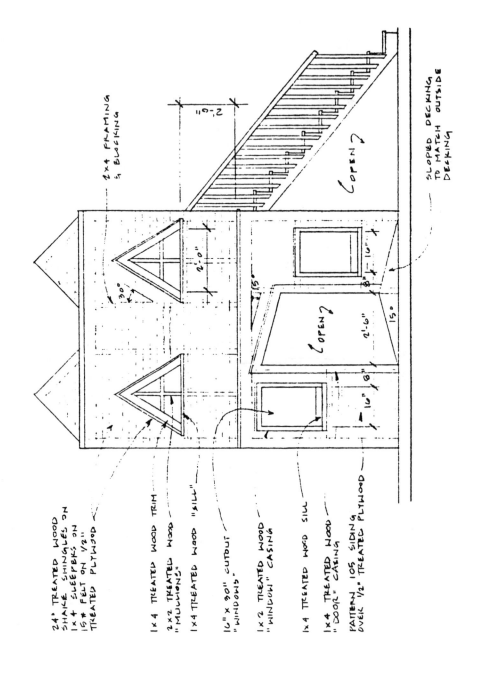

ELEVATION B

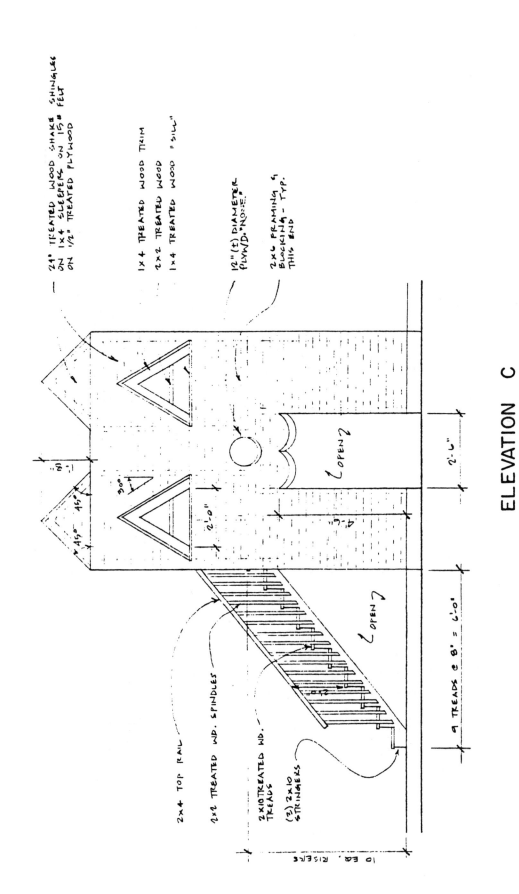

24" TREATED WOOD SHAKE SHINGLES ON 1x4 SLEEPERS ON 15# FELT ON 1/2" TREATED PLYWOOD

1x4 TREATED WOOD TRIM

2x2 TREATED WOOD

1x4 TREATED WOOD "SILL"

12" (±) DIAMETER PLYWD. "NOSE"

2x6 FRAMING & BLOCKING - TYP. THIS END

2x4 TOP RAIL

2x2 TREATED WD. SPINDLES

2x10 TREATED WD. TREADS

(3) 2x10 STRINGERS

30°

45°

45°

2'-0"

2'-0"

4'-3"

2'-6"

OPEN

OPEN

9 TREADS @ 8" = 6'-0"

10 EA. RISERS

ELEVATION C

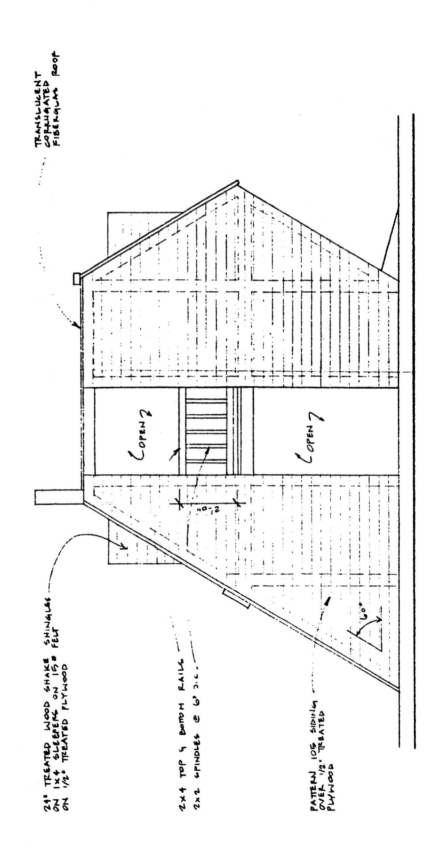

TRANSLUCENT CORRUGATED FIBERGLASS ROOF

24" TREATED WOOD SHAKE SHINGLES ON 1x4 SLEEPERS ON 15# FELT ON 1/2" TREATED PLYWOOD

(OPEN)

(OPEN)

2x4 TOP & BOTTOM RAILS
2x2 SPINDLES @ 6" O.C.

PATTERN 105 SIDING OVER 1/2" TREATED PLYWOOD

60°

ELEVATION   D

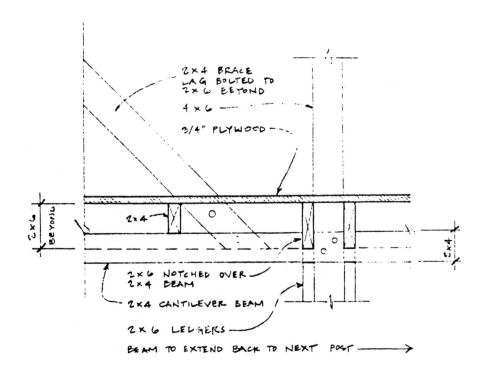

2×4 BRACE
LAG BOLTED TO
2×6 BEYOND

4 × 6

3/4" PLYWOOD

2×4

2×6 BEYOND

2×4

2 × 6 NOTCHED OVER
2 × 4 BEAM

2×4 CANTILEVER BEAM

2 × 6 LEDGERS

BEAM TO EXTEND BACK TO NEXT POST ⟶

DETAIL 'E'

VICTORIAN PLAY HOUSE

Designed by Kathy Smith Anthenat

This elegant 8′×8′ Victorian-style play house includes a porch with sturdy railing, a wood door with an oval window, and an old-fashioned screen door. Two screened windows extend low enough to provide cool breezes for children who prefer to sit on the floor while playing. The doors are extra wide to allow the structure to be used for storage during the winter months. The exposed 2×4 framework inside is painted white to reflect sunlight up to a cozy loft, which is large enough for two adults to sleep in. The yellow and white play house pictured cost $1,000 to build.

Children use a wood ladder to climb up to the loft (you can make one with wood dowels and 2×4s). Place the ladder at a slight incline (bottom about 12″ out from wall) on the same side of the front wall as the handle for the wood door. This will allow the door to be opened flat against the opposite side. Securely fasten the ladder to the floor and top plate with four 2″ corner braces. If your child is quite young, you may want to wait until he or she is older before adding the ladder—for safety reasons. In the meantime the loft can be used as a storage area. Also, if the loft will be used for slumber parties, a guardrail should be added to the open edge to prevent someone from accidentally rolling off during the night.

BILL OF MATERIALS

patio blocks or a poured foundation
14—treated 2″×4″×8′
28—treated 1″×4″×8′
4—treated 4″×4″×6′
48—2″×4″×8′
2—1″×6″×8′
27—1″×4″×8′
2—1″×4″×10′
5—1″×3″×8′
1—1″×2″×4′
5—4′×8′ sheets ¾″ CDX plywood
6—4′×8′ sheets ⅝″ T-111 4″ o.c. siding
1—4′×8′ sheets ¼″ lauan plywood
½″×8″ beveled redwood siding to cover 20 square feet
5—4″×33″×½″ spindle rail
16—5½″×5½″×½″ decorative brackets
21′ of ¹¹⁄₁₆″ quarter round
22′ of ¾″ square moulding
43′ of ¾″ cove moulding
16′ of ¼″×¾″ flat screen moulding
2—19⅞″×46⅞″ double track storm windows
1 square roof shingles
roofing felt—20″×32″
clear acrylic sheet
screen wire—2½′×5½′
4—2½″ flat corner braces
32—1½″ corner braces
4—2″ corner braces
2—magnetic catches (for doors)
2—3½″ hinges (for wood door)
3—1½″ hinges (for screen door)
4—drawer pulls to use as door handles
wood ladder
wood putty
paint
fasteners:
    corrugated nails
    wood screw
    plated wood screws
    brads
    wood glue

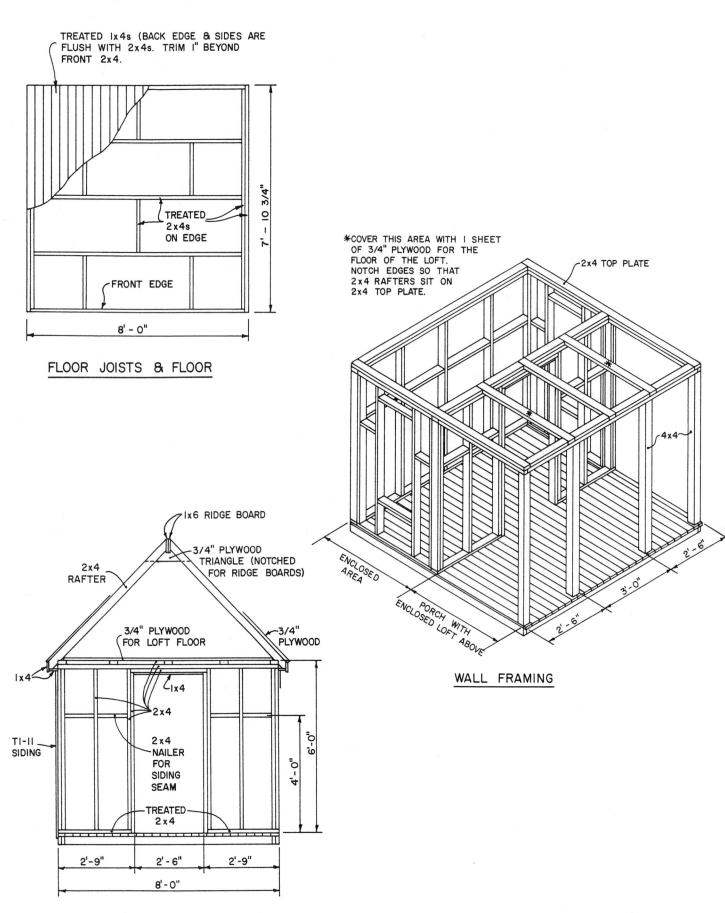

TREATED 1x4s (BACK EDGE & SIDES ARE FLUSH WITH 2x4s. TRIM 1" BEYOND FRONT 2x4.

7' - 10 3/4"

TREATED 2x4s ON EDGE

FRONT EDGE

8' - 0"

FLOOR JOISTS & FLOOR

*COVER THIS AREA WITH 1 SHEET OF 3/4" PLYWOOD FOR THE FLOOR OF THE LOFT. NOTCH EDGES SO THAT 2x4 RAFTERS SIT ON 2x4 TOP PLATE.

2x4 TOP PLATE

4x4

ENCLOSED AREA

PORCH WITH ENCLOSED LOFT ABOVE

2' - 6"

3' - 0"

2' - 6"

WALL FRAMING

1x6 RIDGE BOARD

3/4" PLYWOOD TRIANGLE (NOTCHED FOR RIDGE BOARDS)

2x4 RAFTER

3/4" PLYWOOD FOR LOFT FLOOR

3/4" PLYWOOD

1x4

1x4

2x4

T1-11 SIDING

2x4 NAILER FOR SIDING SEAM

TREATED 2x4

6' - 0"

4' - 0"

2' - 9"

2' - 6"

2' - 9"

8' - 0"

FRONT WALL FRAMING CROSS-SECTION

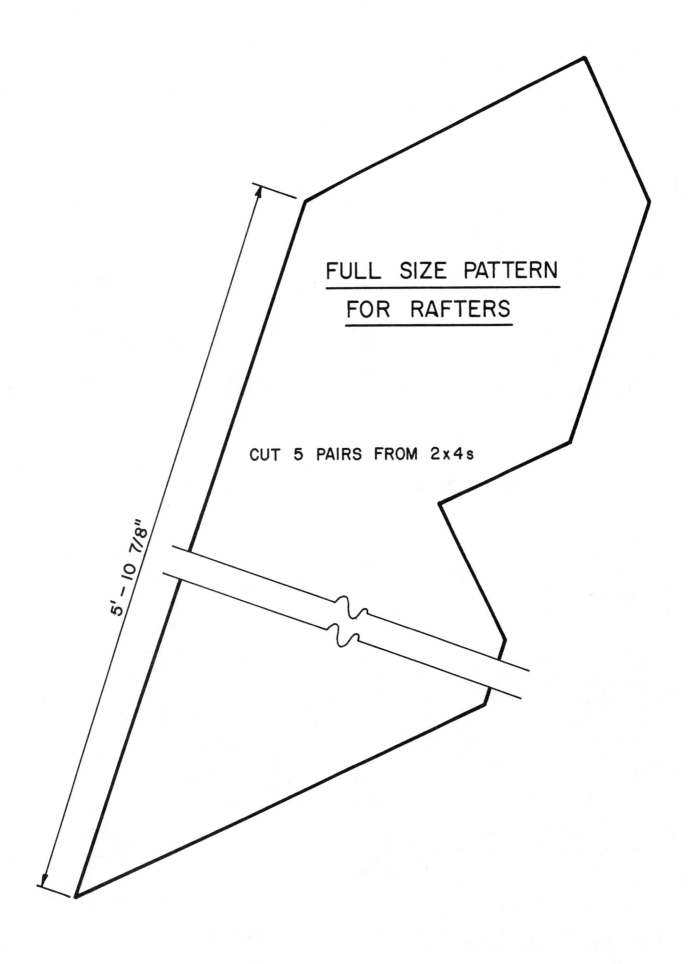

FULL SIZE PATTERN

FOR RAFTERS

CUT 5 PAIRS FROM 2x4s

5'-10 7/8"

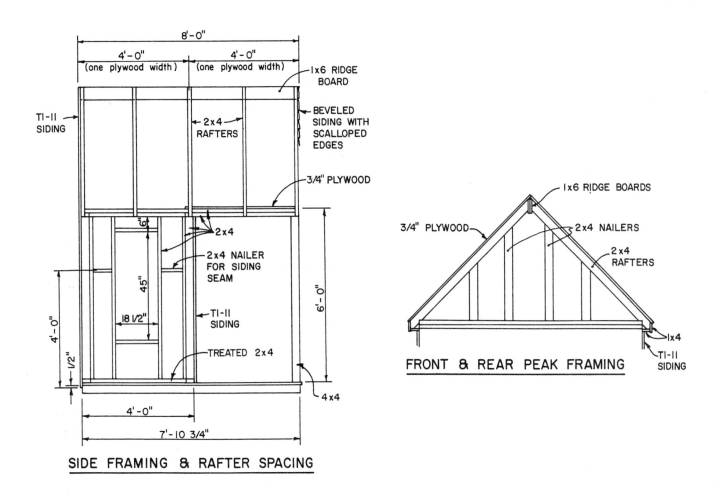

SIDE FRAMING & RAFTER SPACING

8'-0"

4'-0" (one plywood width) 4'-0" (one plywood width)

1x6 RIDGE BOARD

BEVELED SIDING WITH SCALLOPED EDGES

TI-11 SIDING

2x4 RAFTERS

3/4" PLYWOOD

6"

2x4

2x4 NAILER FOR SIDING SEAM

45"

TI-11 SIDING

18 1/2"

4'-0"

1/2"

TREATED 2x4

6'-0"

4x4

4'-0"

7'-10 3/4"

FRONT & REAR PEAK FRAMING

1x6 RIDGE BOARDS

3/4" PLYWOOD

2x4 NAILERS

2x4 RAFTERS

1x4

TI-11 SIDING

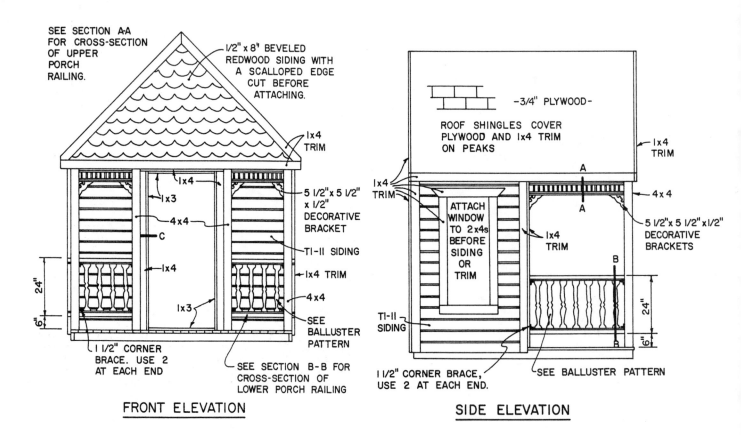

FRONT ELEVATION

SEE SECTION A-A FOR CROSS-SECTION OF UPPER PORCH RAILING.

1/2" x 8" BEVELED REDWOOD SIDING WITH A SCALLOPED EDGE CUT BEFORE ATTACHING.

1x4 TRIM

1x4

1x3

4x4

C

1x4

1x3

5 1/2" x 5 1/2" x 1/2" DECORATIVE BRACKET

TI-11 SIDING

1x4 TRIM

4x4

SEE BALLUSTER PATTERN

24"

6"

1 1/2" CORNER BRACE. USE 2 AT EACH END

SEE SECTION B-B FOR CROSS-SECTION OF LOWER PORCH RAILING

SIDE ELEVATION

-3/4" PLYWOOD-

ROOF SHINGLES COVER PLYWOOD AND 1x4 TRIM ON PEAKS

1x4 TRIM

A

A

1x4 TRIM

4x4

1x4 TRIM

ATTACH WINDOW TO 2x4s BEFORE SIDING OR TRIM

1x4 TRIM

5 1/2" x 5 1/2" x 1/2" DECORATIVE BRACKETS

B

TI-11 SIDING

B

24"

6"

1 1/2" CORNER BRACE, USE 2 AT EACH END.

SEE BALLUSTER PATTERN

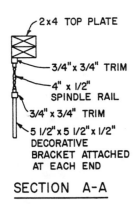

2x4 TOP PLATE

3/4" x 3/4" TRIM

4" x 1/2" SPINDLE RAIL

3/4" x 3/4" TRIM

5 1/2" x 5 1/2" x 1/2" DECORATIVE BRACKET ATTACHED AT EACH END

SECTION A-A

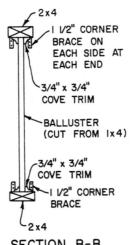

2x4

1 1/2" CORNER BRACE ON EACH SIDE AT EACH END

3/4" x 3/4" COVE TRIM

BALLUSTER (CUT FROM 1x4)

3/4" x 3/4" COVE TRIM

1 1/2" CORNER BRACE

2x4

SECTION B-B

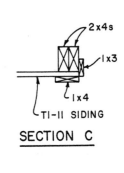

2x4s

1x3

1x4

TI-11 SIDING

SECTION C

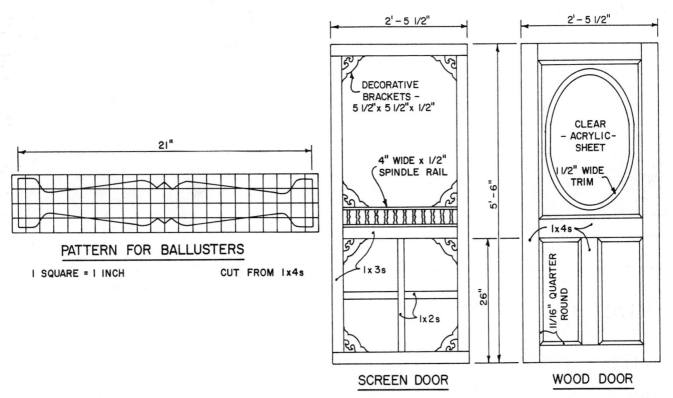

21"

PATTERN FOR BALLUSTERS

1 SQUARE = 1 INCH   CUT FROM 1x4s

2'-5 1/2"

DECORATIVE BRACKETS - 5 1/2"x 5 1/2"x 1/2"

4" WIDE x 1/2" SPINDLE RAIL

1x3s

1x2s

5'-6"

26"

SCREEN DOOR

2'-5 1/2"

CLEAR -ACRYLIC- SHEET

1 1/2" WIDE TRIM

1x4s

11/16" QUARTER ROUND

WOOD DOOR

NOTES -
SCREEN DOOR - Use 2 1/2" flat corner braces & corrugated nails on back side. Attach screen wire to back side and cover edges with 1/4"x 3/4" flat screen moulding.
WOOD DOOR - Cut 5'-6" x 2'-5 1/2" lauan plywood base for door and cut an oval the size of the inner oval shown above in it. Cut a 1 1/2" wide oval ring for outer trim as shown. Cut another ring 3/4" wide and an oval of clear acrylic to fit inside this ring. Paint wood rings before assembly. A border design can be etched on the window with an electric pencil engraver. Assemble with wood glue & screws. Use wood putty for a finished look on outer ring edge.

TEPEE

Instructions by Kathy Smith Anthenat

This simplified tepee makes a great play house for all ages. It is "simplified" because the collar-like flaps that American Indians would have added at the top of their tepee dwellings have been omitted here.

The 12' high tepee shown here is made from a 12' × 24' rectangle of 8 oz. canvas. If you do not wish to make one this large, just keep in mind that your canvas must be twice as long as it is wide (for instance 6' × 12') so that it makes a square when folded in half. The door opening and top hole dimensions would remain the same as for the 12' tepee.

If local stores do not carry the size canvas you need, copy down the address of the manufacturer of the canvas they do carry and write to the company for a price quote. Inform them that you do not need the canvas hemmed, nor do you need grommets. Another option is to sew together two or more pieces of canvas to get the size you need.

Expenses for this tepee were kept to a minimum—$81 for the canvas, twine, and wood dowels. Poles were obtained for free from nearby woods (with the landowner's permission), and the paint used was left over from other projects.

BILL OF MATERIALS

12' × 24' 8 oz. (or heavier) canvas
14' long poles (at least 9)
Latex paint thinned with water
Brown poly twine
7/16" wood dowels
Pegging stakes
Heavyduty thread

INSTRUCTIONS

1 Find a flat area large enough to lay the canvas out smooth when folded in half to make a 12' square—perhaps the garage or driveway. With a pencil lay out the tepee covering as shown below. The easiest way to make the large radius for the bottom edge of the tepee covering is to have one person hold one end of a string on the corner which is the center of the circle and another person draw the edge with a pencil held 12' down the string.

Cut through both thicknesses of canvas to make a semi-circle. The door flap—which is optional—is

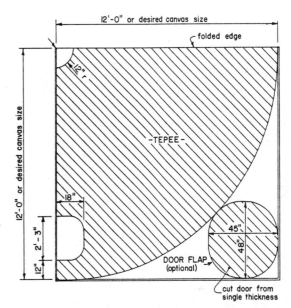

cut from a single thickness. Note: The remaining scraps of canvas can be sewn together to make a storage bag for the tepee.

2 Hem all edges to prevent fraying.

3 Lay the tepee covering out flat as shown below, with front edges overlapped. When the tepee is smoothed out, the bottom will overlap more than the top. Be sure the top overlaps by at least 6".

With a pencil, draw on the fastening holes as shown. Punch holes through both layers with a nail or an ice pick. Place the door flap (if you are making one) in position covering the doorway, and punch holes to match the two sets of holes just above the

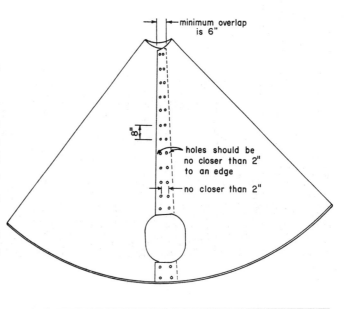

doorway.

Draw a ⅟₁₆″ diameter circle and a ¾″ diameter circle around each hole. Use scissors to cut the hole at the top, bottom, and each side out to the ⅟₁₆″ circle line. Use an overcast stitch and heavy-duty thread to outline the hole from the inner circle to the outer circle (like a button hole). Check to make sure the ⅟₁₆″ wood dowels can slide through the finished holes.

4 Sew loops of twine around the bottom edge of the tepee covering at 2′ intervals. To make the loops, cut twine in 1′ lengths, tie in a knot, and securely sew to the tepee. These will be used to hold the bottom edge of the canvas securely to the ground.

5 Paint designs as desired on the exterior side of the canvas with thinned latex paint. Let dry thoroughly.

6 Cut ⅟₁₆″ wood dowels (available at craft or building supply stores) into 12″ long pieces. You will need fourteen for the 12′ tepee. Paint dark brown.

7 To erect the tepee, lay three poles flat on the ground as shown and tie together. If you do not have access to small trees to use for poles, you might find tall bamboo poles at a gardening center or home improvement store. Or use PVC pipe which has been painted brown. The pipe can be connected with couplers if necessary to obtain the needed length.

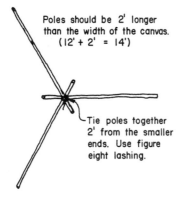

Poles should be 2′ longer than the width of the canvas. (12′ + 2′ = 14′)

Tie poles together 2′ from the smaller ends. Use figure eight lashing.

8 Raise the junction of the poles off the ground 3′ or 4′. Wrap the canvas covering around them as shown and fasten the upper edges together with dowel rods. These holes will be too high to reach on a 12′ tepee when the poles are completely erected.

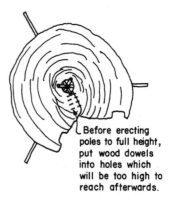

Before erecting poles to full height, put wood dowels into holes which will be too high to reach afterwards.

9 With one person on each pole, raise the junction of the poles to what you think is about the right height. Fasten together a set of holes in the center of the covering and a set at the bottom to see whether the bottom ends of the poles are out too far or in too far. Adjust as necessary.

10 Add more support poles; the more poles, the rounder the tepee.

11 Insert the rest of the wood dowels. Make any final adjustments of the poles so that the canvas is stretched smooth and tight. The optional door flap is held on by the two dowels above the door opening. Sew a 3′ length of twine to the tepee on either side of the door opening—at the top—for holding the door flap when rolled up.

12 Cut pegging stakes as shown for holding the bottom of the tepee to the ground. These can be made from the tree tops which were cut off to make the support poles, or you can buy tent stakes. Use one for each twine loop, pounding them securely into the ground to prevent a strong wind from upsetting the tepee.

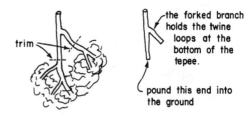

trim

the forked branch holds the twine loops at the bottom of the tepee.

pound this end into the ground

LEAN-TO

Instructions by Kathy Smith Anthenat

Here is a great project for those kids who live in the country and have access to a wooded area with plenty of tall, slender trees. Mom or Dad might want to help construct the framework and leave weaving the foliage covering to the kids.

There are no set dimensions; you make them up as you go along and see what you have to work with.

INSTRUCTIONS

1 Find two trees the desired distance apart and attach a ridge pole. Tie with brown poly twine or rope. Note: All intersections during this construction should be tied. Wrap the twine around the intersection several times before tying tightly.

Save the branches of foliage that are trimmed off any of the poles. They will be used later for the woven covering.

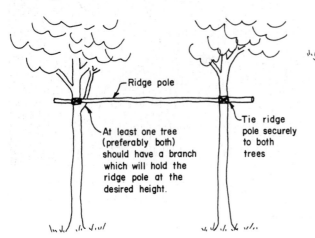

Ridge pole

At least one tree (preferably both) should have a branch which will hold the ridge pole at the desired height.

Tie ridge pole securely to both trees

2 Add the end leaning poles. One end is sharpened and pushed into the ground. Make sure the poles are the same length.

End leaning poles

Leave nubs when trimming branches. These can be used later to help hold horizontal poles.

3 Add more leaning poles. They should be no more than 14″ apart.

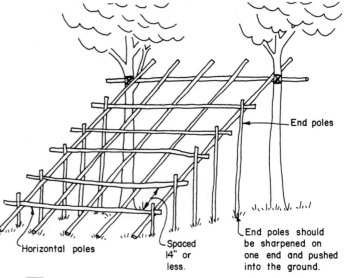

Spaced 14″ or less

4 Add end poles and horizontal poles. Remember that all intersections should be tied securely. If the horizontal poles are flexible enough you can weave them through the leaning poles.

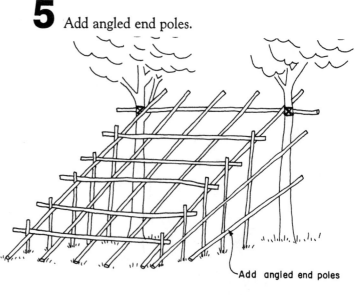

End poles

Horizontal poles

Spaced 14″ or less.

End poles should be sharpened on one end and pushed into the ground.

5 Add angled end poles.

Add angled end poles

6 Weave leafy branches through the frame, starting at the bottom. Overlap them for a thick, waterproof roof.

If desired, the opening at the front can be narrowed by framing a section of it with horizontal and vertical poles.

The cut ends of the leafy branches used for weaving a covering should point up and out so they won't poke children playing inside the lean-to.

Challenge your sons or daughters (if they are old enough) to make a chair like this one in the woods with only a bucksaw and a ball of twine!

GRASS HUT

Designed by Kathy Smith Anthenat

The backside of this grass hut has not yet been covered with grass bundles. Freshly picked wildflowers edge the doorway and window.

Add this shaggy grass hut to your landscaping scheme for a conversation piece as well as a play house. It stands approximately 6½' high and is 5' in diameter—large enough for an adult to enter, yet cozy enough to fulfill a child's desire for a private space of his or her own. Since the major building material is grass, this unique play house is very inexpensive—$36 for the one pictured.

For an educational bonus, check out a book from the library to show your son or daughter pictures of grass huts that people in other cultures have made for their families to live in. Although those grass huts most likely did not have wire fence frames (yours will), constructing a grass hut will be a fascinating learning experience for everyone. Depending on the age of your children, you can assign them the tasks of cutting, tying, or carrying the required grass bundles—dozens of them! They will very likely be surprised at how many bundles it takes to cover even a structure this small.

Making the wire frame is a job for adults only; there are too many ways for a child to get hurt when cutting and forming wire. Wear safety goggles at all times to protect yourself from flying pieces of wire, especially when cutting out cross wires in preparation for fastening two edges together.

Although the wire frame should be sitting in the desired final location before tying on the grass covering, you might want to construct it in a more convenient place, such as your garage. Two adults can easily move the completed frame to its permanent location.

BILL OF MATERIALS

30' of 14 gauge, 4' high, 1" × 2" welded wire fence
Several balls of brown poly twine
Tall grass (at least 1½' long)

INSTRUCTIONS

Wire Frame

1 With wire clippers, cut off about 16' of fence. Overlap the ends a few inches; fasten together as shown. This will give you a 4' high circle of wire.

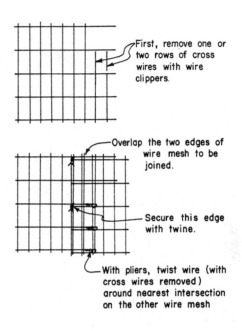

First, remove one or two rows of cross wires with wire clippers.

Overlap the two edges of wire mesh to be joined.

Secure this edge with twine.

With pliers, twist wire (with cross wires removed) around nearest intersection on the other wire mesh

Be sure while constructing the frame that no wire tips are left poking upward, downward, or toward the interior of the hut where they might scratch or otherwise injure a child. After any twisting and fastening, the tips ends should be pointing slightly outward, where they will be well padded with layers of grass later. Also, for a nice looking finished interior, make all twine knots on the exterior side of the frame where they will be hidden by the next higher layer of grass.

2 Cut a piece of wire fence about 20" wide and 10' long to begin making the dome top. This first piece will overlap each side by about 8" to make a sturdy arch to work off of for the rest of the dome. Fasten as shown. The top of this wire arch should be approximately 6½' from the ground. The remaining pieces of fence used for the dome do not need to overlap the base this much.

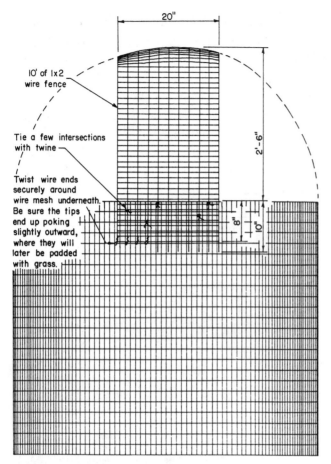

20"

10' of 1x2
wire fence

2'-6"

Tie a few intersections
with twine

Twist wire ends
securely around
wire mesh underneath.
Be sure the tips
end up poking
slightly outward,
where they will
later be padded
with grass.

8"
10"

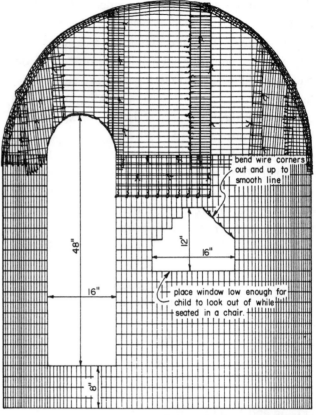

bend wire corners
out and up to
smooth line

48"

12"

16"

16"

place window low enough for
child to look out of while
seated in a chair.

8"

3 Continue cutting off pieces of wire and bending as necessary to form a sturdy dome shape. Tie overlapping intersections here and there to help keep the dome shape and to increase the rigidity of the structure. All wire ends should be securely fastened to the wire mesh underneath. Since some of these ends will be easier to twist from the inside, do what you can from the outside and save the rest until a doorway is cut.

Don't be concerned if the dome top is "lumpy." The bumps will not be noticeable after the grass covering is attached.

4 Use wire clippers to cut a doorway and window opening. The removed sections of wire can be used to fill in gaps in the dome top.

This fencing form is ready to be covered with grass bundles.

Grass Covering

1 To make finished edges around the door and window openings, outline them with small handfuls of grass as shown. Do not pack these edges too tightly; you will need to poke twine through them when adding layers of grass in Step 2. Trim the outlining grass neatly as shown.

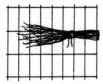

Bend small handfuls of grass over the edge of the opening. Tie with brown poly twine.

2 Cut large handfuls of grass and tie as shown.

Grass bundles should be tied 2 1/2 – 3" from the cut ends. Wrap twine around it at least three times and tie in a double knot. Leave 6" of string hanging for tying the bundle onto the wire frame.

3 Tie the bundles to the exterior side of the frame — starting at the bottom and working your way up. How far apart or close together the bundles need to be will depend on how long and bushy the grass is. The grass should be plush enough to hide the wire frame completely. Generally, each higher row should cover half the length of the grass bundle beneath it.

When you get up to the rounded tops of the doorway and window, tie the grass bundles on high enough that the bushy tips hang even with the upper edge of the opening. This will look nicer than keeping the bundle tops in rows and cutting the grass afterwards to match the window line.

The grass bundles for the center of the top of the hut need to be double-ended. Cut a large handful of grass and divide into two handfuls. Place half the cut ends facing one direction and half facing the other direction. Tie in the center for a bundle with two bushy ends. Make enough double-ended bundles to cover all the cut ends and knots on the top of the hut. A smooth, rounded top will shed rain water.

The grass outlining the doorway has already been trimmed.

SOUTHERN PINE PLAY HOUSE

Courtesy of the Southern Pine Marketing Council

Courtesy of Southern Forest Products Association.

This 6′×6′ play house—constructed with durable, pressure treated Southern Pine—will be around to delight more than one generation of youngsters.

BILL OF MATERIALS

To build this playhouse you will need the following quantities of CCA pressure treated Southern Pine lumber:

# of Pieces	Material	Length	Preservative Retention Level
3	4"×6"	8'	.40 lbs./cu. ft.
8	4"×4"	8'	.40 "
6	2"×6"	12'	.40 "
4	2"×4"	10'	.40 "
2	2"×6"	10'	.40 "
8	2"×4"	6'	.25 "
3	1"×6"	10'	.25 "
13	1"×6"	6'	.25 "
9	2"×2"	6'	.25 "

PLUS:

5—4'×8' sheets ½" T-111 treated plywood siding
8d, 10d, 12d, and 16d hot-dipped galvanized nails
2 galvanized standard eave drips, 6' long
Construction adhesive for treated wood
3 galvanized butt hinges, Stanley F1798P or equivalent
Door handle and closure hardware of your choice
Water repellent sealer
Roof materials (to cover 65 sq. ft.)
    Fiberglass or asphalt shingles
    15 lb. roofing felt
    Roofing nails
    Sheathing plywood, 3 sheets, 4'×8', ½" thick

Tools required:

✓ Circular or crosscut saw
✓ Square
✓ Hammer
✓ Screwdriver
✓ Stakes, line, level
✓ Carpenter's rule or tape

INSTRUCTIONS

1 Determine exact location of playhouse. Cut one 4×6 skid to 7'0" and the other two to 7'6" long.

Arrange the two longer skids beneath door location for step support. Refer to plan for skid placement; position them with the top of the skid flush with ground level. Use stakes, line, and level to aid accurate installation of footer skids.

2 Cut six of the 4×4 posts to 6'3" long. Using 16d nails, toe-nail three each to the outside skids. Use square to maintain true vertical of posts. Likewise, toe-nail the two 8' 4×4 center posts to the center skid. Refer to plan for post spacing.

3 Stabilize the posts by attaching the double 2×4 rafter supports to the tops of 6'3" posts. Use four of the 6' 2×4s. Attach with 10d nails and construction adhesive.

4 Cut one 12' 2×6 in half. Square up all 4×4 posts by attaching 2×6 top brace at front and rear. Top edge of this member should be flush with the top of the double 2×4 rafter support. Attach to posts using 12d nails and construction adhesive. Check for square and level.

5 From the 10' 2×6 material, cut two pieces 6'3" long; use the leftovers for two of the window sills, each 30¾" long. From one of the 12' 2×6s, cut one piece 6'0" long and two more window sills. From another 12' 2×6, cut one piece 6'0" long, one window sill, and the other front step.

6 Attach two 6'0" 2×6s to three 4×4 posts on each side. Bottom edge of 2×6 should be 3" above 4×6 skid. Use 12d nails and construction adhesive.

7 Complete lower perimeter frame by attaching two 6'3" 2×6s at front and rear. Use 12d nails and construction adhesive. Make sure entire frame remains level and square. Outside dimension of lower 2×6 frame should be 6'3" on a side.

8 Cut the remaining 12' 2×6s in half for the six floor joists. Refer to plan for placement; attach to posts and frame using 10d nails and construction adhesive.

9 Build the 2 × 2 subframe to receive ½″ treated plywood siding and window sills. Recess subframe 1″ from the exterior side of 4 × 4 posts. Attach 2 × 2 material to 4 × 4 posts using 10d nails and construction adhesive. At windows, finished subframe height should be 2′5″ above top of floor joists.

10 Cut 10′ 1 × 6 material to 8′8″. Trim ends according to plan for "cottage look." Use 8d nails to toe-nail 1 × 6 ridge board in place atop 4 × 4 center posts.

11 Cut eight 2 × 4 rafters from the 10′ lengths. Refer to plan for roof pitch, overhang dimension and the notch to fit the 2 × 4 rafter support. Using 10d nails, toe-nail rafters in place, 2′0″ on center. End rafters should be flush with the ends of the rafter support.

12 Attach 1 × 6 fascia to rafter ends using 8d nails and construction adhesive.

13 Using the 6′ 1 × 6 boards, attach floor boards to 2 × 6 joists using 8d nails and construction adhesive. Cut notches to fit around 4 × 4 posts and subframe where needed. Floor board ends should be flush with outside edge of 2 × 2 subframe.

14 Cut treated plywood siding panels to fit between 4 × 4 posts. Attach to subframe using 8d nails and construction adhesive.

15 Also from the treated siding, cut triangular panels to fit gable, covering top of 4 × 4 center posts and end rafters. Attach panels to these members using 8d nails and construction adhesive.

16 Install the roof, noting 6″ overhang front and rear. Use 8d nails to attach ½″ sheathing plywood to rafters. Sheathing should just cover the top edge of the 1 × 6 fascia boards. Add a layer of roofing felt. Attach galvanized eave drips to ends of sheathing plywood; use 8d nails. Attach shingles with roofing nails.

17 Build the door. Cut a piece of the treated plywood siding 2′5″ wide by 5′0″ high. Construct 2 × 4 door frame according to the plan, with finished outside dimension of 2′5″ by 4′11″. Attach frame to the unfinished side of plywood panel; use 8d nails and construction adhesive. Top edge of frame should remain flush, leaving 1″ of plywood at the bottom to clear floor boards when door is closed. Refer to plan. Hang door on 4 × 4 corner posts using 3 galvanized hinges and screws. Close door to locate position of a 2 × 2 door stop on the 4 × 4 post opposite the hinges. Cut a piece of 2 × 2 material and attach it to the post using 10d nails and construction adhesive. Add your choice of a door knob, centering it at 3′4″ from the bottom of the door.

18 Attach 2 × 6 window sills to 2 × 2 subframe using 10d nails and construction adhesive. Slope each sill ¼″ to the outside. Toe-nail one 10d nail to each adjoining 4 × 4 post to secure sloping position.

19 Construction is complete. Apply a coat of water repellent sealer to all exposed surfaces.

NOTES

√ Hot-dipped galvanized or stainless steel nails and fasteners should be used.

√ Fasten horizontal members (deck boards, stair treads) "bark side up"; note the direction of annual rings.

√ When nailing toward the end of the boards, predrilling holes or blunting nail points is recommended.

√ Sawing should be done outdoors while wearing a dust mask.

√ Eye goggles should also be worn when power sawing or machining.

√ When construction is completed, the application of a water repellent sealer is recommended.

√ Treated wood scraps should be disposed of by ordinary trash collection, they should not be burned.

√ Clothing accumulating sawdust from treated wood products should be laundered before re-use and washed separately from other household clothing.

√ Areas of skin in contact with treated wood should be thoroughly washed before eating, drinking, or using tobacco products.

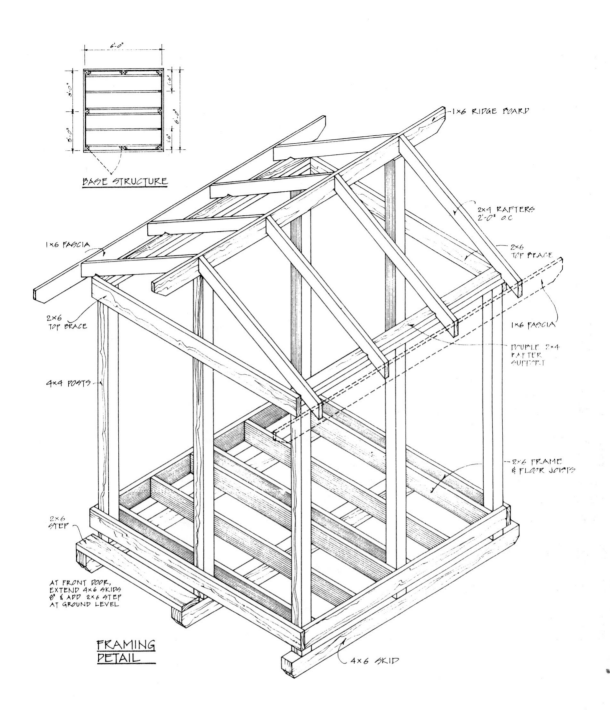

6'-0"

3'-0"

5'-0"

BASE STRUCTURE

1×6 RIDGE BOARD

2×4 RAFTERS
2'-0" O C

1×6 FASCIA

2×6
TOP BRACE

1×6 FASCIA

2×6
TOP BRACE

DOUBLE 2×4
RAFTER
SUPPORT

4×4 POSTS

2×6 FRAME
& FLOOR JOISTS

2×6
STEP

AT FRONT DOOR,
EXTEND 4×6 SKIDS
8" & ADD 2×6 STEP
AT GROUND LEVEL

FRAMING
DETAIL

4×6 SKID

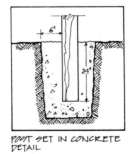

6"

24"

POST SET IN CONCRETE
DETAIL

PLAYHOUSE

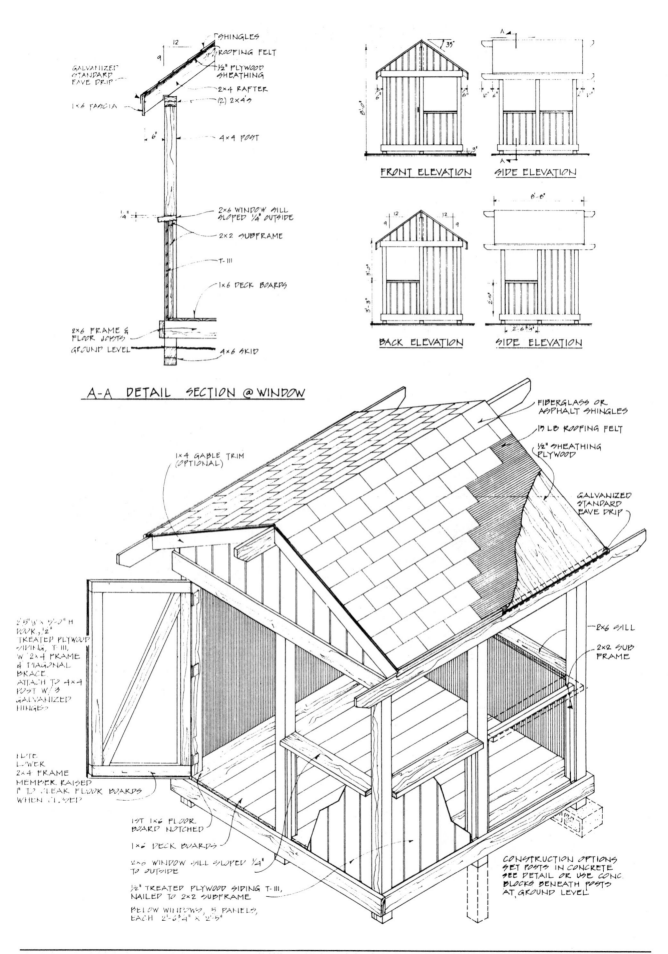

SHINGLES
ROOFING FELT
½" PLYWOOD SHEATHING
GALVANIZED STANDARD EAVE DRIP
2×4 RAFTER
(2) 2×4's
1×6 FASCIA
4×4 POST
6"
2×6 WINDOW SILL SLOPED ¼" OUTSIDE
2×2 SUBFRAME
T-III
1×6 DECK BOARDS
2×6 FRAME & FLOOR JOISTS
GROUND LEVEL
4×6 SKID

A-A DETAIL SECTION @ WINDOW

FRONT ELEVATION

SIDE ELEVATION

BACK ELEVATION

SIDE ELEVATION

FIBERGLASS OR ASPHALT SHINGLES
15 LB ROOFING FELT
½" SHEATHING PLYWOOD
GALVANIZED STANDARD EAVE DRIP

1×4 GABLE TRIM (OPTIONAL)

2'-6" W × 5'-0" H DOOR, ½" TREATED PLYWOOD SIDING, T-III, W/ 2×4 FRAME & DIAGONAL BRACE. ATTACH TO 4×4 POST W/ 3 GALVANIZED HINGES

NOTE: LOWER 2×4 FRAME MEMBER RAISED 1" TO CLEAR FLOOR BOARDS WHEN CLOSED

1ST 1×6 FLOOR BOARD NOTCHED

1×6 DECK BOARDS

2×6 WINDOW SILL SLOPED ¼" TO OUTSIDE

½" TREATED PLYWOOD SIDING T-III, NAILED TO 2×2 SUBFRAME BELOW WINDOWS, 5 PANELS, EACH 2'-6¾" × 2'-5"

2×6 SILL

2×2 SUB FRAME

CONSTRUCTION OPTIONS SET POSTS IN CONCRETE SEE DETAIL OR USE CONC. BLOCKS BENEATH POSTS AT GROUND LEVEL

TOURIST CABIN

Courtesy of The University of Tennessee Agricultural Extension Service

This cabin would make a great play house or club house now and a guest cottage later. The clothes closet could be fitted with removable shelves for storing games, volleyball nets, etc.

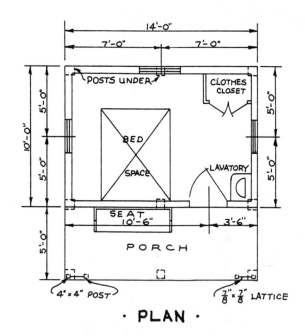

· PLAN ·

14'-0"
7'-0" · 7'-0"
10'-0"
5'-0" · 5'-0" · 5'-0" · 5'-0"
5'-0"

POSTS UNDER
CLOTHES CLOSET
BED SPACE
LAVATORY
SEAT 10'-6"
3'-6"
PORCH
4"×4" POST
$\frac{7}{8}$"×$\frac{7}{8}$" LATTICE

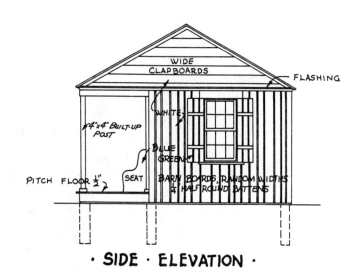

· SIDE · ELEVATION ·

WIDE CLAPBOARDS
FLASHING
4"×4" BUILT-UP POST
WHITE
BLUE GREEN
PITCH FLOOR 1$\frac{1}{2}$"
SEAT
BARN BOARDS, RANDOM WIDTHS & HALF ROUND BATTENS

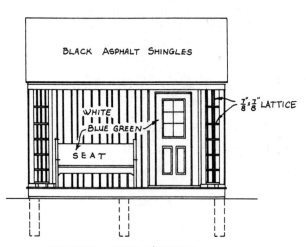

· FRONT · ELEVATION ·

BLACK ASPHALT SHINGLES
WHITE
BLUE GREEN
SEAT
$\frac{7}{8}$"×$\frac{7}{8}$" LATTICE

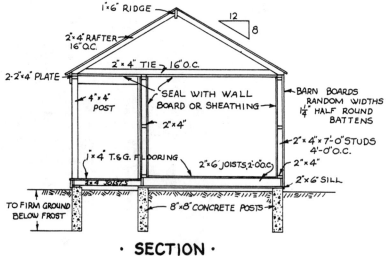

· SECTION ·

1"×6" RIDGE
12
8
2"×4" RAFTER 16" O.C.
2"×4" TIE 16" O.C.
2-2"×4" PLATE
4"×4" POST
SEAL WITH WALL BOARD OR SHEATHING
2"×4"
BARN BOARDS RANDOM WIDTHS 1$\frac{1}{4}$" HALF ROUND BATTENS
2"×4"×7'-0" STUDS 4'-0" O.C.
1"×4" T.& G. FLOORING
2"×6" JOISTS 2'-0" O.C.
2"×4"
2"×4" JOISTS
2"×6" SILL
TO FIRM GROUND BELOW FROST
8"×8" CONCRETE POSTS

FOUR PERSON TOURIST CABIN

Courtesy of The University of Tennessee Agricultural Extension Service

What a wonderful place for sleepovers and summer fun. When the children have grown, it can become a beautiful guest cottage, workshop, or winter storage area for patio furniture. It was originally designed to sleep four, but you might want to use the berths—without mattresses—as game, craft, and storage spaces. The lower berth could also be hinged, with a large, enclosed storage area below.

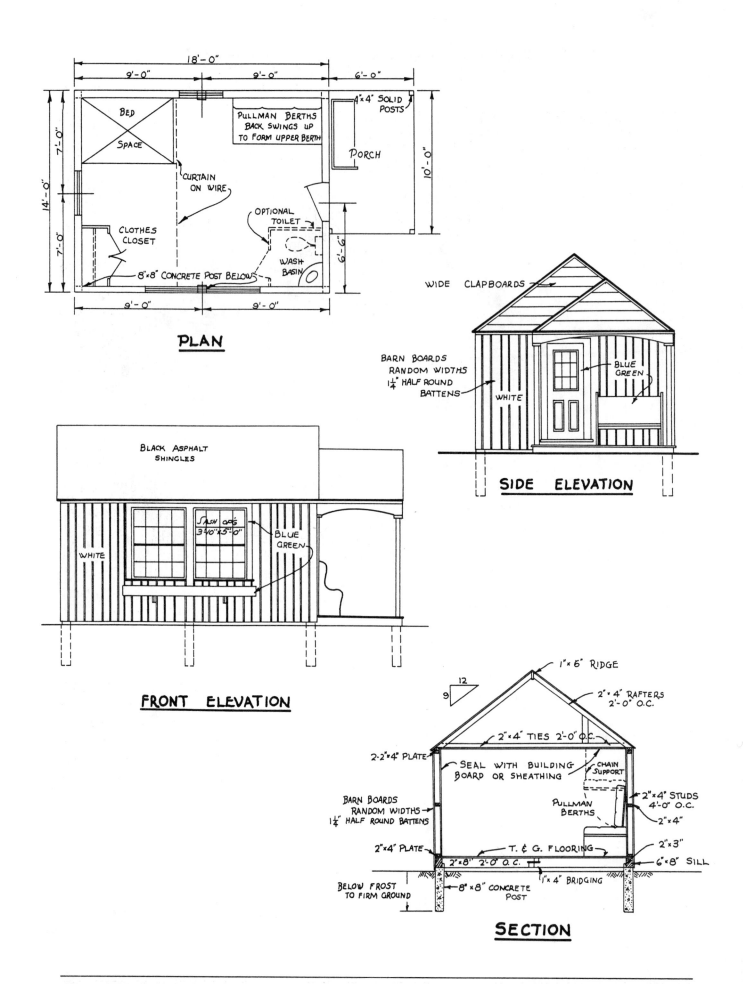

PLAN

FRONT ELEVATION

SIDE ELEVATION

SECTION

PVC PIPE PLAY HOUSE

Designed by Kathy Smith Anthenat

This versatile little play house complete with a table and two chairs was built for under $100. It is lightweight and portable for moving around the yard when mowing or for moving from one home to the next for those families on the go. Children can use it as a stage for performing plays, or for holding neighborhood pet shows. Modify the covering and it becomes a stable for a nativity scene. Need to construct a games booth for a children's club or organization? This fits the bill in style!

This play house will never need painting and will not rust or rot. It is sturdy enough to withstand rain and wind, and at 5′ tall will also fit in your basement. By using screws instead of PVC cement to attach the side and top lengths of pipe to the front and rear panels, the play house can be stored flat when not in use.

WARNING: Because this play house is so light-weight, you must anchor it to the ground in some way when it is being used outdoors so that the wind will not catch it and send it flying to possibly hurt some-one. It can be anchored in various ways, including tying twine to the bottom joints to hold them firmly to the ground with tent stakes. DO NOT ALLOW CHILDREN NEAR THIS PLAY HOUSE UNLESS IT IS FIRMLY ANCHORED WHEN OUTDOORS.

BILL OF MATERIALS

	Rear Panel	Top & Sides	Front Panel	Table	Two Chairs	TOTAL
pipe, 1 1/2"			4		8	12
pipe, 2"	4				8	12
pipe, 3"	3					3
pipe, 4"			2			2
pipe, 6 1/4"			2			2
pipe, 7"				4	8	12
pipe, 9 1/2"	2		2		8	12
pipe, 11"				4		4
pipe, 12"					4	4
pipe, 19 1/4"			2			2
pipe, 20 3/4"			2			2
pipe, 25"				2		2
pipe, 30"			2	2		4
pipe, 34 3/4"	6					6
pipe, 38"	2					2
pipe, 40"			2			2
pipe, 41"	1					1
pipe, 60"		2				2
pipe, 62"		5				5

(Total of 13 lengths of 3/4" pipe, 10" long)

	Rear Panel	Top & Sides	Front Panel	Table	Two Chairs	TOTAL
end caps	3		2	4	8	17
cross	1					1
outlets	2		2			4
adapters	2		2			4
tees	10		9	4	16	39
45 elbows			4			4
90 elbows				4	8	12
pipe clips				4	8	12

3/4" or 1" plywood - one @ 31" x 28 1/2" and two @ 14" x 10 1/2"
10 yards 45" wide striped fabric
4 yards 45" wide polka dot fabric
sixteen 3/4" round velcro fasteners
1 can PVC cement, 2 cans PVC cleaner

INSTRUCTIONS

Pipe

1 Remove manufacturer's printing from the ¾" pipe with PVC cleaner.

2 Cut pipe to required lengths (see Bill of Materials) using a plastic tube cutter or a hacksaw in a miter box. Remove any burrs from cut ends with medium-grit sandpaper.

3 Pre-assemble pipe and fittings according to drawings *without cement* to be sure everything fits properly. Reassemble with cement following directions on back of cement can.

Note: If you want to store this play house flat when not in use, fasten the 60″ and 62″ lengths of pipe to the front and rear panels using wing screws instead of cement. To do this, after the front and rear panels have been permanently assembled with cement, insert the top and side lengths of pipe in place without cement. Drill small holes through these fitting and pipe joints (only to center, not through the other side) and insert wing screws. To make lining up these holes easier the next time the play house is assembled, draw a line across both the fitting and the pipe and label with a permanent marker (A—A, B—B,...). You need only label and line the screw joints on the rear panel; the front holes will automatically line up if the rear ones are lined up.

Wood Tops

1 Scraps left over from another project work great for the table top and seats. Cut out to required size, rounding off the corners. Sand all surfaces smooth. Paint to match colors in fabric. (The table in the photographs has a green and white checkerboard pattern painted in the center of the table, and a scalloped green border painted around the edges. The chair seats are also painted with green and white checkerboard patterns.) A coat of clear exterior finish can be added for protection against the weather and crayon marks.

2 Attach top and seats to the table and chairs (which have already been assembled with cement) using pipe clips and screws.

Fabric

1 A variety of fabrics can be used. The stripes and polka-dot combination is a natural for kids. Or you may have some old tablecloths, sheets, or tarps that you want to use. Cut out fabric as shown in FABRIC LAYOUT diagram.

2 The "A" pieces form the two sides. For each side, sew together selvage edges of two "A" pieces for a center seam. With an iron, press under a 1″ hem along all four sides; press under 1″ again to make a double thickness 1″ hem. Topstitch ⅛″ and ⅞″ from the edge.

3 Repeat Step 2 with the "B" pieces for the back.

4 Repeat Step 2 with the "E" pieces for the top.

5 Match sets of "C" pieces so that the stripes run up and down on the two finished triangles. With right sides together sew two triangle pieces together. Leave an opening to turn the triangle inside out. Turn right side out and press. Topstitch ⅛″ and ⅞″ from edges.

6 Sew together strips of "F" pieces to total 210″ (same as "D" piece). Press seams flat. Put right sides of "D" and "F" pieces together; sew ends and scalloped edge. Turn right side out and press. Fold inside 1″ of the top edge on both pieces of fabric and press. Sew top edge ⅛″ from edge and ⅞″ from edge. Topstitch along scalloped edge.

7 Insert eyelet into each corner and at the center seam of the top, side, and back rectangles. Also, insert an eyelet in the center of the hem on the short sides of the top rectangle and at each point on the triangles.

8 Using sturdy twine, tie these pieces in their proper places on the play house. There should be gaps between the fabric and the pipe for the wind to blow through.

9 Using a cyanoacrylate-type glue (Super Glue™) attach the hook-and-loop fasteners along the top pipes and fittings of the play house. The scalloped border does not cover the rear of the play house, so have a friend help you hold the border in place to see where the last fastener on each side should be glued. Once the glue has dried, hold the border in place and glue or sew the other side of the fastener to the top edge of the fabric.

FRONT PANEL (exterior side)

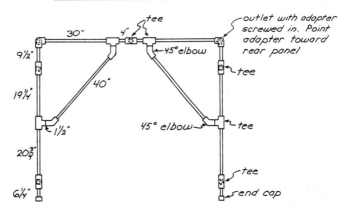

REAR PANEL (interior side)

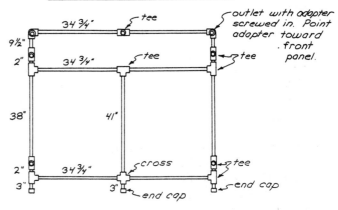

Front and rear panels are connected with two 60″ lengths of pipe (insert between adapters) and five 62″ lengths of pipe.

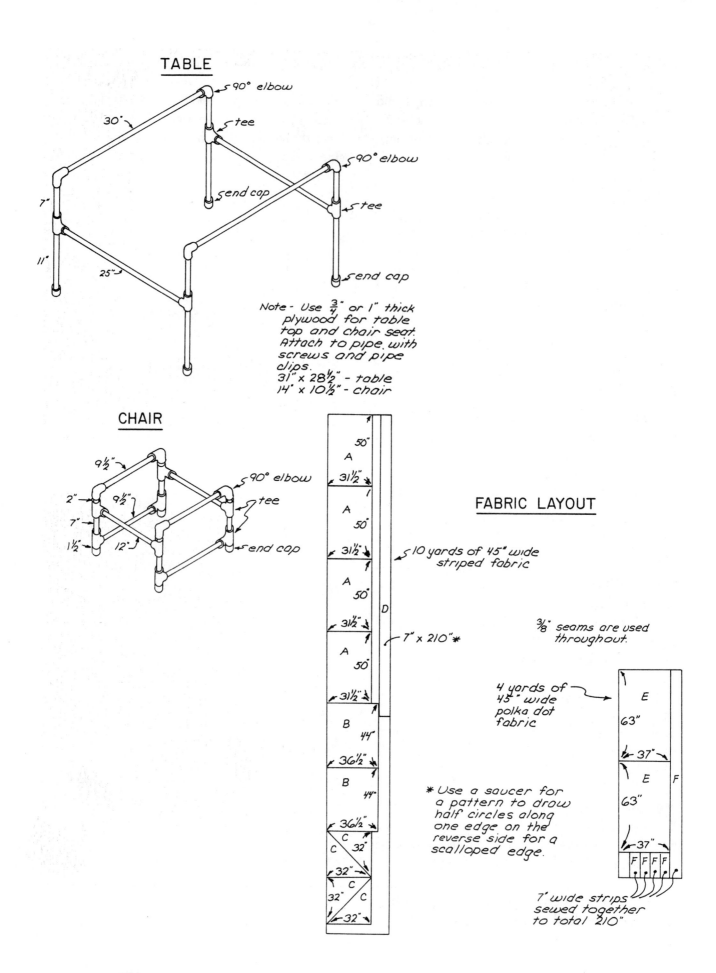

TABLE

90° elbow

30"

tee

90° elbow

7"

end cap

tee

11"

25"

end cap

Note - Use 3/4" or 1" thick plywood for table top and chair seat. Attach to pipe with screws and pipe clips.
31" x 28½" - table
14" x 10½" - chair

CHAIR

9½"

2"

9½"

90° elbow

tee

7"

1½"

12"

end cap

FABRIC LAYOUT

50"

A

31½"

A

50"

31½"

A

50"

D

31½"

7" x 210" *

A

50"

31½"

B

44"

36½"

B

44"

36½"

C

C   32"

32"

C

32"   C

32"

10 yards of 45" wide striped fabric

3/8" seams are used throughout.

4 yards of 45" wide polka dot fabric

E

63"

37"

E

63"

F

37"

F F F F

* Use a saucer for a pattern to draw half circles along one edge on the reverse side for a scalloped edge.

7" wide strips sewed together to total 210"

While mom has a garage sale, the children turn this play house into a profitable refreshment stand.

The PVC Pipe Play House canopy makes a moveable shade for the baby while letting the breeze flow through.

HOMEWISE PLAYHOUSE/STORAGE SHED

Adapted with permission from plans produced by Homewise, Inc., Copyright 1992.

Courtesy of Al Wasco, Housing Resource Center.

BILL OF MATERIALS

24 — 2″ × 4″ × 5′
7 — 2″ × 4″ × 6′
10 — 2″ × 4″ × 8′
1 — 2″ × 2″ × 8′
4 — 1″ × 2″ × 6′
6 — 1″ × 3″ × 6′
4 — 1″ × 4″ × 6′
1 — 1″ × 4″ × 3′
1 — 4′ × 8′ ¾″ CDX plywood
2 — 4′ × 8′ ½″ waferboard
Roofing Material: 32 sq. ft. to be covered
Siding: 80 sq. ft. to be covered
Fasteners, Hardware:
8 — ¼″ × 3″ carriage bolts with washers
4 — ¼″ × 3½″ carriage bolts with washers
4 — ¼″ × 2½″ carriage bolts with washers
10 — 3″ angle irons
one pair 2½″ gate hinges for door
3 pounds — 6d galvanized common nails
3 pounds — 10d sinker nails
2 pounds — 1″ roofing nails
Tools:
    Circular saw
    Electric drill and ¼″ bit
    Combination square
    Tape measure
    Screwdriver
    Hammer

INSTRUCTIONS

Note: All framing is made with 2 × 4 material nailed with 10d sinker nails. If sinker nails are not available, use common nails.

1 Platform.
Cut and nail 2 × 4s as shown. Use 10d sinker nails. Cut ¾″ CDX plywood 48″ × 67″. Nail with 6d galvanized nails about 8″ apart.

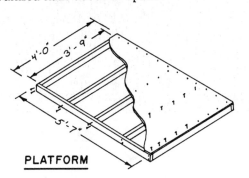

PLATFORM

2 Front and Back.
Cut and nail 2 × 4 framing as shown.

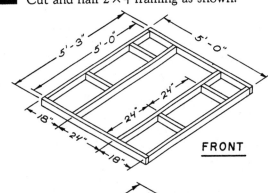

FRONT

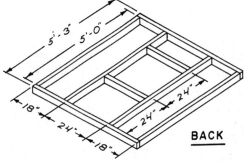

BACK

3 Ends.
Cut and nail 2 × 4 framing as shown. Make two ends.

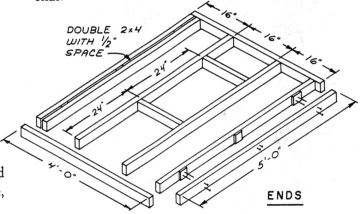

ENDS

4 Put up walls.
Stand front panel on platform, centered (3½″ in from each end). Drill and bolt to platform as shown, using 3″ carriage bolts.

Next, assemble back panel, then two ends in similar fashion, bolting to platform.

Install 3″ angle irons to each top inside corner to hold panels together.

Last, cut 2 × 4 section out of bottom of doorway and nail to top 2 × 4.

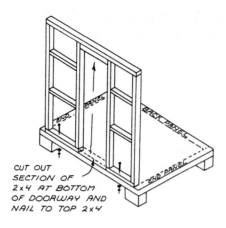

WALL ASSEMBLY

CUT OUT SECTION OF 2×4 AT BOTTOM OF DOORWAY AND NAIL TO TOP 2×4

5 Roof.
First, look at ROOF ASSEMBLY drawing below to see how it's put together; then cut ten pieces of 2×4—30" long as shown. Use PATTERN FOR ENDS for angle on both ends of each 2×4.

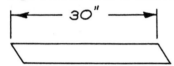

← 30" →

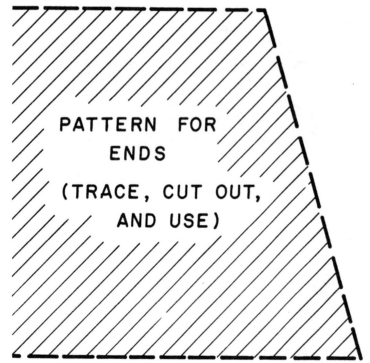

PATTERN FOR ENDS (TRACE, CUT OUT, AND USE)

Nail these to 6' 1×4s to make 2 roof panels. The 2×4 at each end is 2½" in; the rest are spaced evenly. Use 6d galvanized nails.

Cut two pieces of ½" waferboard, 31"×72". Nail to roof panels, using roofing nails about 8" apart. The front edge overhangs the 1×4 about ¾".

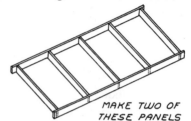

MAKE TWO OF THESE PANELS

ROOF PANEL

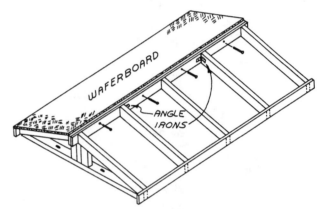

WAFERBOARD

ANGLE IRONS

ROOF ASSEMBLY

6 Roof Supports.
Cut and nail as shown, using 2×4 material. Make two.

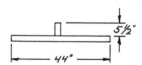

5½"
44"

Lay these on top of end walls, then set roof panels on top. Temporarily clamp or nail center 1×4s, then drill and bolt with 2½" carriage bolts as shown in ROOF ASSEMBLY.

Slide supports to touch roof rafter and mark angles on ends. Cut ends, then add additional pieces as shown in ROOF SUPPORT DETAIL.

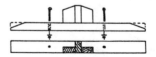

ROOF SUPPORT DETAIL

Reinstall supports and drill and bolt in place, using 3½″ carriage bolts. Add angle irons as shown in ROOF DETAIL (VIEW FROM INSIDE).

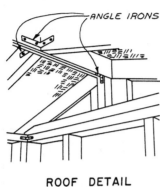

ROOF DETAIL
(VIEW FROM INSIDE)

Install roofing. Use shingles (two bundles) or 90# roll roofing.

7 Finish Walls.
You can cover the framing with a variety of materials — we used 8″ Abitibi fiberboard siding. You can also use waferboard or T-111 plywood. Use 2 × 2s for back-up nailers as needed. If you want to be able to take the play house apart, be sure to nail siding to only one of the walls at the corners, not both.

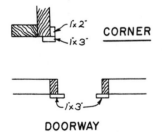

For corner moulding we used 1 × 3 and 1 × 2 strips, and 1 × 3 strips at the doorway.

8 Door.
Cut a piece of ¾″ plywood 23¾″x23¾″. Set a piece of ¼″ scrap under door bottom, then press door

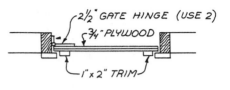

DOOR DETAIL

against 1 × 3 casing and against 2 × 4 stud on left. Fasten 2½″ gate hinges with strap on back of door. Mount hinges about 2″ from top and bottom.

Mark lines on face of door about ⅛″ from both 1 × 3 casings, then use 1 × 2s or 1 × 3s to create a decorative pattern within these lines.

9 Other Ideas.
√ Use scrap wood to make window sills and/or mouldings.
√ Put window screen on gable ends for ventilation (or use gable vents).
√ Add small lift-up windows or shutters for rainy days.
√ Drill drain holes in platform in case it gets wet.
√ Add a shelf at top of door to create a play store!
√ Omit windows and build a full door for use as a storage shed.

TRADITIONAL 8' × 12' PLAY HOUSE

Designed by Kathy Smith Anthenat

The exterior of this basic 8' × 12' structure can be finished in many different styles; two are shown here. The play house includes a porch, a loft area above the porch, and an 8' × 8' room—large enough for a guest cottage or an office after the children have grown. Three pairs of windows and a door provide ample ventilation.

Because the structure can be finished in a variety of ways, no Bill of Materials is given. The example with the "PATRICK'S WORKSHOP" sign uses V-groove siding, 8" o.c., and only one section of porch railing to give the porch an open feeling. The railing uses 2 × 4s for the top and bottom rail and 2 × 2s for the balusters.

The other example uses T-111 siding, 4" o.c., applied horizontally. A more cozy feeling is obtained by using three sections of porch railing. (Refer to the baluster pattern and porch railing detail for construction details.)

NOTES

√ This structure should be constructed on a poured foundation or patio blocks.

√ Cover the ¾" plywood roof with roofing felt and asphalt shingles.

√ All studs and rafters are left exposed on the inside. This gives children a chance to use left-over scraps of wood to build shelves between the 2 × 4s.

√ If the loft will be used for a sleeping area you should add a railing along the open edge to guard against someone falling off the ledge during the night.

√ A wood ladder is used for access to the loft—you can construct one from 2 × 4s and wood dowels. Attach it securely to the floor and the top plate along the open edge of the loft with four 2" corner braces.

√ If desired, small windows could be added at the peaks for additional ventilation.

TREATED 1x6 T & G FLOORING. BACK EDGE AND SIDES ARE FLUSH WITH 2x4s. TRIM FRONT EDGE 1" BEYOND FRONT 2x4.

TREATED 2x4s ON EDGE

11' - 10 3/4" (ASSUMING 5/8" SIDING IS USED)

FRONT EDGE

8'-0"

FLOOR JOISTS & FLOOR

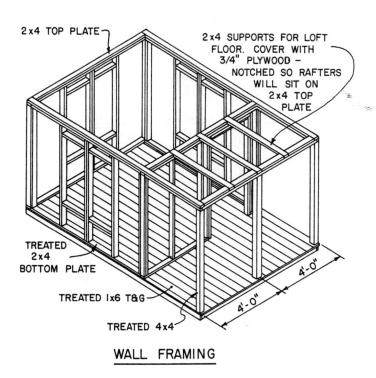

2x4 TOP PLATE

2x4 SUPPORTS FOR LOFT FLOOR. COVER WITH 3/4" PLYWOOD — NOTCHED SO RAFTERS WILL SIT ON 2x4 TOP PLATE

TREATED 2x4 BOTTOM PLATE

TREATED 1x6 T&G

TREATED 4x4

4'-0"

4'-0"

WALL FRAMING

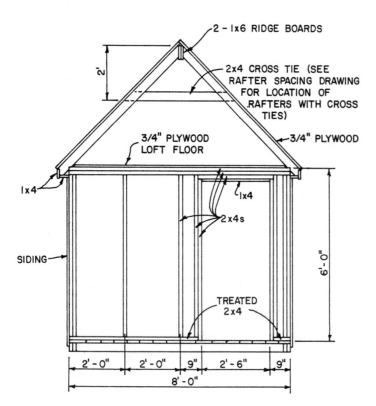

FRONT WALL FRAMING CROSS-SECTION

2 – 1x6 RIDGE BOARDS

2x4 CROSS TIE (SEE RAFTER SPACING DRAWING FOR LOCATION OF RAFTERS WITH CROSS TIES)

3/4" PLYWOOD LOFT FLOOR

3/4" PLYWOOD

1x4

1x4

2x4s

SIDING

TREATED 2x4

2'

6'-0"

2'-0" 2'-0" 9" 2'-6" 9"

8'-0"

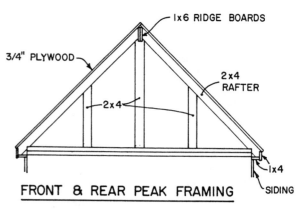

FRONT & REAR PEAK FRAMING

1x6 RIDGE BOARDS

3/4" PLYWOOD

2x4 RAFTER

2x4

1x4

SIDING

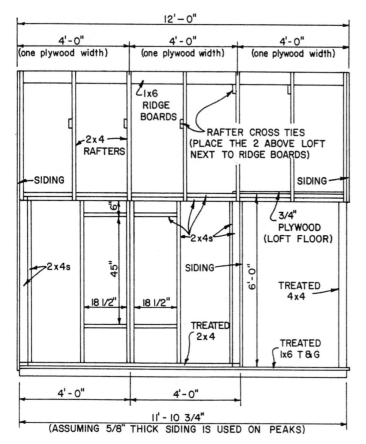

SIDE FRAMING AND RAFTER SPACING

12'-0"

4'-0" (one plywood width)   4'-0" (one plywood width)   4'-0" (one plywood width)

1x6 RIDGE BOARDS

RAFTER CROSS TIES (PLACE THE 2 ABOVE LOFT NEXT TO RIDGE BOARDS)

2x4 RAFTERS

SIDING

SIDING

2x4s

3/4" PLYWOOD (LOFT FLOOR)

6"

45"

18 1/2"   18 1/2"

2x4s

SIDING

TREATED 2x4

6'-0"

TREATED 4x4

TREATED 1x6 T&G

4'-0"   4'-0"

11'-10 3/4"

(ASSUMING 5/8" THICK SIDING IS USED ON PEAKS)

NOTE:
If placing 4x8 sheets of siding horizontally you will need to add horizontal 2x4s to the wall framing to nail the siding seam to. Center two windows on each side wall and the back wall. Use DOUBLE TRACK STORM WINDOWS, 19 7/8" x 46 7/8".

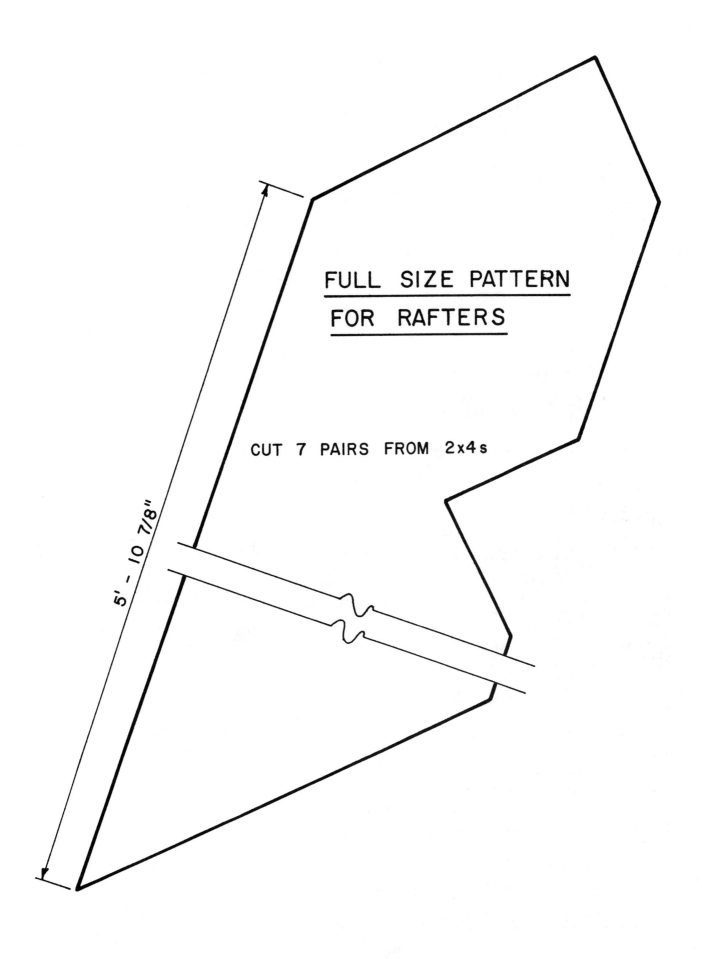

FULL SIZE PATTERN

FOR RAFTERS

CUT 7 PAIRS FROM 2x4s

5' - 10 7/8"

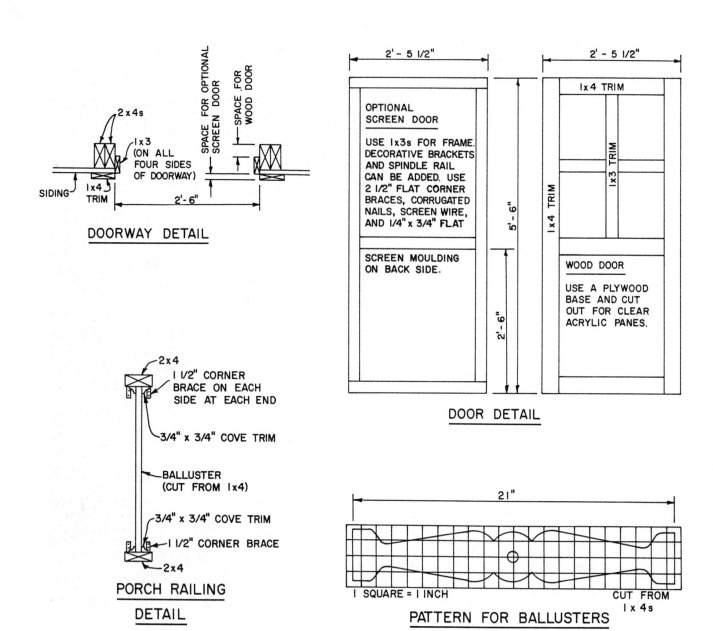

2 x 4s

1 x 3
(ON ALL
FOUR SIDES
OF DOORWAY)

SIDING

1 x 4
TRIM

SPACE FOR OPTIONAL SCREEN DOOR

SPACE FOR WOOD DOOR

2'- 6"

DOORWAY DETAIL

2x4

1 1/2" CORNER
BRACE ON EACH
SIDE AT EACH END

3/4" x 3/4" COVE TRIM

BALLUSTER
(CUT FROM 1x4)

3/4" x 3/4" COVE TRIM

1 1/2" CORNER BRACE

2x4

PORCH RAILING
DETAIL

2'- 5 1/2"

OPTIONAL
SCREEN DOOR

USE 1x3s FOR FRAME.
DECORATIVE BRACKETS
AND SPINDLE RAIL
CAN BE ADDED. USE
2 1/2" FLAT CORNER
BRACES, CORRUGATED
NAILS, SCREEN WIRE,
AND 1/4" x 3/4" FLAT

SCREEN MOULDING
ON BACK SIDE.

5'- 6"

2'- 6"

2'- 5 1/2"

1x4 TRIM

1x3 TRIM

1x4 TRIM

WOOD DOOR

USE A PLYWOOD
BASE AND CUT
OUT FOR CLEAR
ACRYLIC PANES.

DOOR DETAIL

21"

1 SQUARE = 1 INCH

CUT FROM
1 x 4s

PATTERN FOR BALLUSTERS

DOWEL DOODLES PLAY HOUSE

Designed by Kathy Smith Anthenat

This medieval castle can easily and quickly be transformed into a fort, a closed room, a tunnel, or anything else in your child's imagination. Each square is self-contained, making assembly and disassembly simple and the design possibilities limitless.

This play house is designed to accommodate two favorite activities of children: putting things together and taking things apart. Like doodles drawn in the margins of a paper, a Dowel Doodles Play House starts out as a square here and a square there—connected and added to until you end up with a puppet theater, or a castle, or a cave with a long tunnel for the entrance, or whatever the imagination conjures up. No matter what the creation, it can be taken apart and stored quite compactly when playtime is over.

There are only three components of this design—connectors, wood dowels, and fabric rectangles. Make as many pieces as you like. The bigger the set, the more options for styles of play houses. A basic rectangular play house which is three squares high, three squares wide, and two squares deep (with one square open for a window, two squares open for a doorway, and a roof) will require 42 connectors, 75 wood dowels, and 33 fabric rectangles. It will measure 57″ × 57″ × 38″ and cost approximately $70.

INSTRUCTIONS

Wood Dowels

Buy 7/16″ diameter wood dowels, 36″ long. They will probably cost less at a building supply store than at a craft store. Cut each dowel in half to make two 18″ long dowels. Do not paint the dowels; unpainted wood provides for a better grip than painted wood when inserting them in the connectors.

Connectors

Buy 1 9/16″ × 1 9/16″ square wood stock from a building supply store. Cut into cubes. Drill a 7/16″ diameter hole in the center of each of the six sides of each cube. The holes should be deep enough to almost but not quite touch in the center. Leave enough wood in the center to prevent dowel rods from being pushed all the way through the cube during assembly. Sand if necessary, but do not paint.

Fabric Rectangles

The rectangles can be made of ripstop nylon, taffeta nylon, metro 60, or any similar fabric. Using three different colors of fabric adds color and provides more choices when designing a structure.

Each rectangle requires a piece of fabric 19″ × 23¼″. If you carefully measure 45/46″ wide fabric, it is often actually 46½″ wide—exactly double the 23¼″ dimension required. In this case, 3⅔ yards of the fabric will yield fourteen rectangles.

Press under ½″ along the two 23¼″ sides of the fabric rectangle. Press under ½″ again for a ½″ wide hem. Stitch.

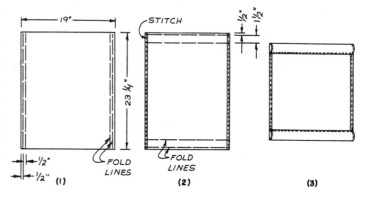

STEPS TO SEWING FABRIC RECTANGLES

This open back puppet theater requires 22 connectors, 35 dowels, and 12 fabric rectangles.

Press under ½" along the two 19" edges. Press under 1½" to form a hem. Stitch close to inner edge. You should now have a hemmed rectangle 17" × 19¼". The wood dowels can be inserted in each end. Note: The fabric rectangles are designed to fit snugly. Make one and check it on a Dowel Doodle square before continuing.

Additional Items

A fun addition to a Dowel Doodles Play House is Dowel Doodles toy furniture for dolls and teddy bears. Children can make a bed, chair, bunk beds, sofa, etc., using the same connectors as used for the play house. Cut the wood dowels to 9" lengths instead of 18". Start with a fabric rectangle 10" by 14¼" (a great way to use up scraps of fabric!) and follow the same hemming instructions as above.

Make a container to store the Dowel Doodles Play House parts by constructing a cube with the connectors and dowels—permanently gluing the parts together—and making a simple fabric lining to go inside.

24' A-FRAME CABIN

Courtesy of the U.S. Department of Agriculture and Purdue University

These plans are for a completely equipped small home, but would make a spacious play house without all the kitchen and bath fixtures, etc. Even if you do not want to include these fixtures now, you might want to put in the basic plumbing and wiring during construction in case you decide to add them later. It would make a wonderful home office after the children are done with it.

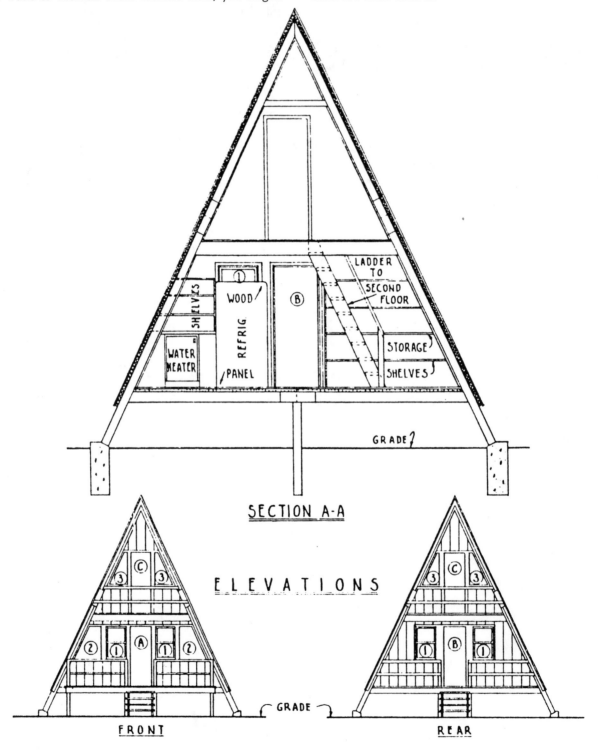

SECTION A-A

ELEVATIONS

FRONT

REAR

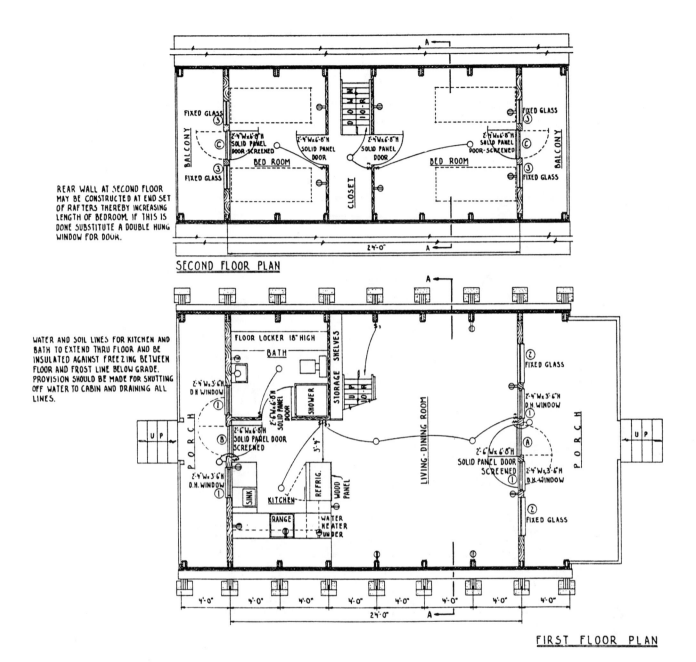

REAR WALL AT SECOND FLOOR
MAY BE CONSTRUCTED AT END SET
OF RAFTERS THEREBY INCREASING
LENGTH OF BEDROOM IF THIS IS
DONE SUBSTITUTE A DOUBLE HUNG
WINDOW FOR DOOR.

SECOND FLOOR PLAN

WATER AND SOIL LINES FOR KITCHEN AND
BATH TO EXTEND THRU FLOOR AND BE
INSULATED AGAINST FREEZING BETWEEN
FLOOR AND FROST LINE BELOW GRADE.
PROVISION SHOULD BE MADE FOR SHUTTING
OFF WATER TO CABIN AND DRAINING ALL
LINES.

FIRST FLOOR PLAN

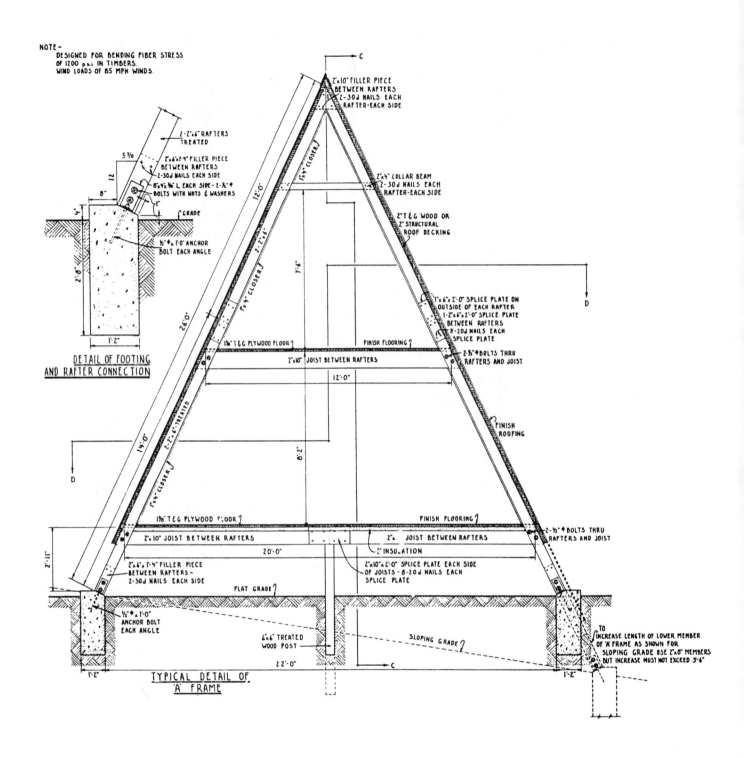

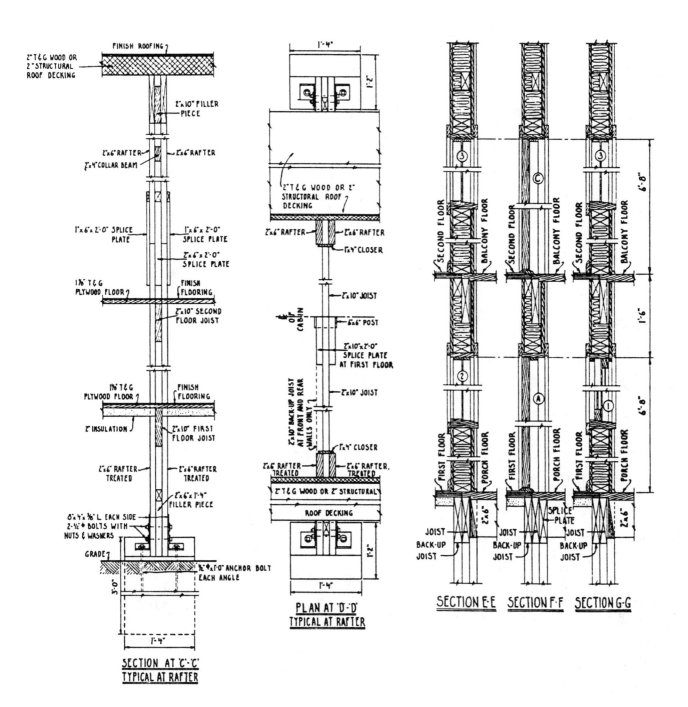

FINISH ROOFING

2" T&G WOOD OR 2" STRUCTURAL ROOF DECKING

2"x10" FILLER PIECE

2"x6" RAFTER   2"x6" RAFTER
2"x4" COLLAR BEAM

1"x6"x2'-0" SPLICE PLATE   1"x6"x2'-0" SPLICE PLATE
2"x6"x2'-0" SPLICE PLATE

1⅛" T&G PLYWOOD FLOOR   FINISH FLOORING
2"x10" SECOND FLOOR JOIST

1⅛" T&G PLYWOOD FLOOR   FINISH FLOORING
2" INSULATION   2"x10" FIRST FLOOR JOIST

2"x6" RAFTER TREATED   2"x6" RAFTER TREATED
2"x6"x1'-4" FILLER PIECE

6"x 4"x ⅜" L EACH SIDE 2-½"⌀ BOLTS WITH NUTS & WASHERS

GRADE

½"⌀x1'-0" ANCHOR BOLT EACH ANGLE

3'-0"

1'-4"

SECTION AT 'C'-'C'
TYPICAL AT RAFTER

1'-4"

1'-2"

2" T&G WOOD OR 2" STRUCTURAL ROOF DECKING

2"x6" RAFTER   2"x6" RAFTER
2"x4" CLOSER

2"x10" JOIST

6"x6" POST

℄ OF CABIN

2"x10"x2'-0" SPLICE PLATE AT FIRST FLOOR

2"x10" JOIST

2"x10" BACK-UP JOIST AT FRONT AND REAR WALLS ONLY

2"x4" CLOSER

2"x6" RAFTER TREATED   2"x6" RAFTER, TREATED

2" T&G WOOD OR 2" STRUCTURAL
ROOF DECKING

1'-2"

1'-4"

PLAN AT 'D'-'D'
TYPICAL AT RAFTER

SECOND FLOOR   BALCONY FLOOR
③

FIRST FLOOR   PORCH FLOOR
②
2"x6"

JOIST
BACK-UP JOIST

SECTION E-E

SECOND FLOOR   BALCONY FLOOR
Ⓒ

FIRST FLOOR   PORCH FLOOR
Ⓐ
SPLICE PLATE

JOIST
BACK-UP JOIST

SECTION F-F

SECOND FLOOR   BALCONY FLOOR
③

FIRST FLOOR   PORCH FLOOR
①
2"x6"

JOIST
BACK-UP JOIST

SECTION G-G

6'-8"

1'-6"

6'-8"

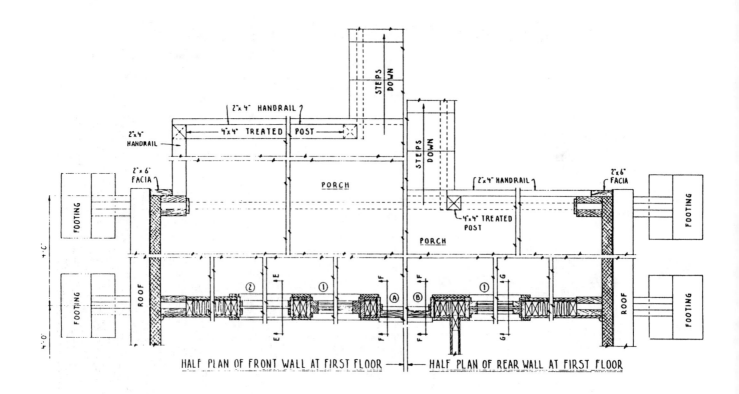

HALF PLAN OF FRONT WALL AT FIRST FLOOR | HALF PLAN OF REAR WALL AT FIRST FLOOR

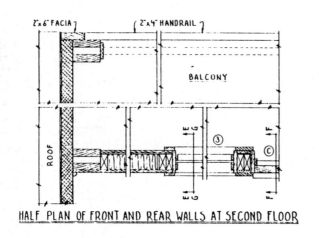

HALF PLAN OF FRONT AND REAR WALLS AT SECOND FLOOR

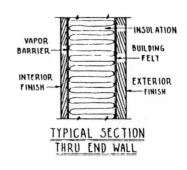

TYPICAL SECTION
THRU END WALL

PENCIL-AND-PAPER PLAY HOUSE

Designed by Kathy Smith Anthenat

This colorful indoor or outdoor play house features "pencil" walls and a "notebook paper" roof. The wall and roof panels can be conveniently constructed in your garage, and then easily assembled at the desired location. Likewise, removing a few screws will allow the panels to be disassembled for easy storage or moving—a definite plus in today's mobile society. This delightful structure stands 5' high, 6' wide, and 31" deep. The model shown was built with an inexpensive grade of pine lumber and cost $170.

The removable double racetrack for mini-cars is a big hit with children of all ages. These tracks can be placed at various angles to the play house to conform to available space. Put the tracks side by side and even large cars and trucks can glide down the incline.

Inside, a total of eight removable shelves—four on each end—provide your child with a place to organize toys and display treasures. Or place them in a row on the upper or lower ledges to form a wider shelf for storing games or stuffed animals.

Every child has little treasures waiting to be proudly displayed on the spacious shelves inside the Pencil-and-Paper Play House.

BILL OF MATERIALS

12 — 1" × 6" × 8'
8 — 1" × 6" × 6'
9 — 1" × 4" × 6'
2 — 1" × 2" × 8'
4 — ¼" × ¾" × 8' flat screen mouldings
1 — 4' × 8' sheet ¼" plywood, finished smooth on both sides
8 — 2½" corner braces
2 quarts of primer
½ pint gloss enamel paint—black
1 quart each of gloss enamel paint—red, green, yellow, blue, white
1¼" screws
¾" × 6" flat head Phillips wood screws
16 × 1½" brads

INSTRUCTIONS

1 From five of the 1×4×6 boards cut four of ROOF FRAME PART A, two of ROOF FRAME PART B, and four SIDE 1×4s. Sand these and the other four 1×4×6s. Paint all pieces yellow.

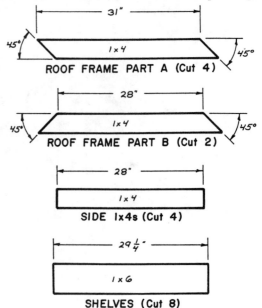

ROOF FRAME PART A (Cut 4)

ROOF FRAME PART B (Cut 2)

SIDE 1x4s (Cut 4)

SHELVES (Cut 8)

FRONT & BACK 1x4s
(4 required — each 6'0" long)

Note: All wood should be painted before assembly. Use one coat of primer and two coats of enamel. Paint both sides and the edges to cover completely. Set aside.

2 Cut one 29¼″ shelf and one 38″ side "pencil" from each of the eight 1 × 6 × 6s. Cut two more side pencils from one of the 1 × 6 × 8 boards for a total of eight shelves and ten side pencils. Sand. Paint shelves yellow. Paint side pencils a variety of red, blue, yellow, and green. Set aside.

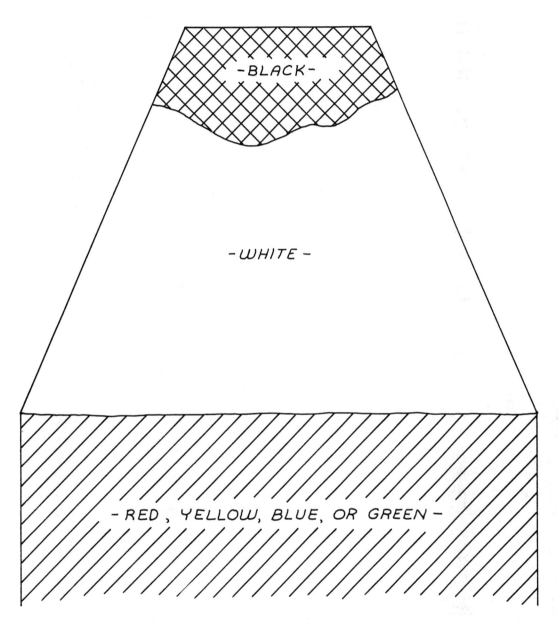

-BLACK-

-WHITE-

- RED , YELLOW, BLUE, OR GREEN -

FULL SIZE PATTERN FOR
TOP OF 1 x 6 'PENCILS'

3 Make two front and back pointed "pencils" from each of the remaining eleven 1×6×8s. They should vary in length, but no pencil should be shorter than 45″. Use the FULL SIZE PATTERN FOR TOP OF 1×6 PENCILS to taper one end of each pencil. To trim for the required 45 degree end angles, equally

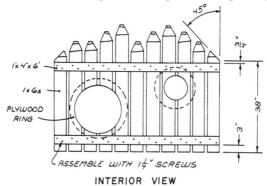

INTERIOR VIEW

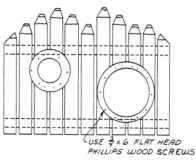

EXTERIOR VIEW

FRONT & BACK ASSEMBLY

space eleven pencils along two of the 1×4×6s as shown in the FRONT & BACK ASSEMBLY drawing. Move them around until you have a pleasing height arrangement. Trim the end pencils (and the ones next to them if necessary) to get the 45 degree angle which begins 38″ from the bottom. Mark what color you want each pencil painted (red, blue, green, or yellow) while they are in position. Repeat with the other eleven pencils. Sand. Paint according to the pattern, but vary the shape of the black tip. Assemble the front and back panels as shown with the screw heads on the interior side. The window and doorway holes will be cut out later.

4 Use the PLYWOOD LAYOUT to cut rings and roof pieces from plywood. (Hint: Drill a hole for a place to start the jigsaw blade.) Sand. Paint the three roof pieces white. Set aside. Paint the four rings

black. Attach to the exterior side of the panels as shown in the FRONT & BACK ASSEMBLY drawing. Use a jigsaw to cut the window and door openings in the pencils. Round off the interior edges of the cut pencils and sand smooth. Paint the edges black.

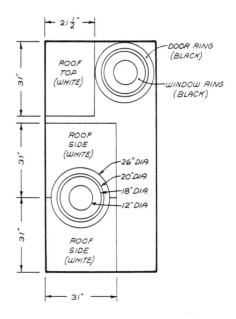

PLYWOOD LAYOUT

5 Connect the front and back panels with the 28″ yellow 1×4s as shown.

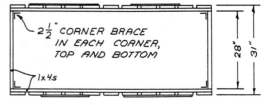

TOP VIEW

6 Evenly space five side pencils on each side and attach as shown. The finished play house will look best if the side pencil is the same color as the pencil it joins on the front or back panel. By attaching the side pencils to the side 1×4s only as shown (and not the end of the front or back panel) the play house can easily be disassembled by removing the screws which hold the corner braces to the front and back panels.

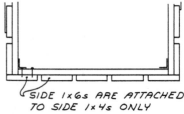

SIDE 1×6s ARE ATTACHED TO SIDE 1×4s ONLY

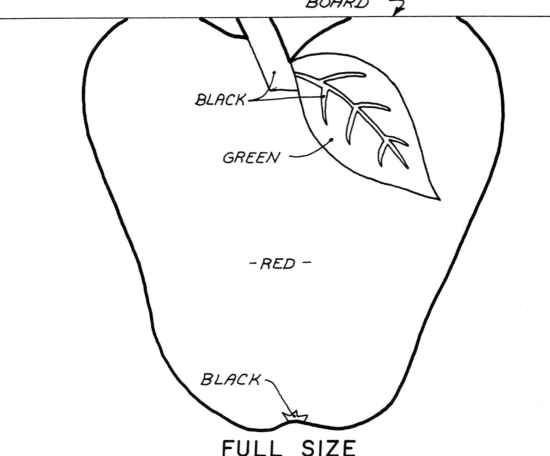

PLACE PATTERN
ON EDGE OF
BOARD

BLACK

GREEN

- RED -

BLACK

FULL SIZE
SHELF SUPPORT PATTERN

7 Cut twelve "apple" shelf supports using the full size pattern and leftover 1×6 or 1×4 scraps. Sand. Paint as shown.

8 Attach six shelf supports on each end of the play house for the two middle shelves as shown. The other shelves lie on the 1×4 ledges. Note: These shelves are designed to be removable so that children can arrange them as desired (they can be placed in a row vertically or horizontally). However, very young children may bump them from underneath and cause them to fall. If you have this problem you can either remove the shelves until the child is older or attach the shelves to the supports or pencils with screws.

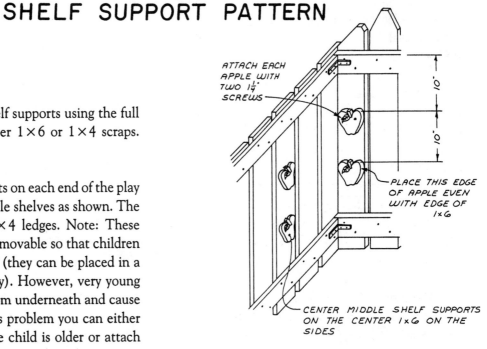

ATTACH EACH APPLE WITH TWO 1¼" SCREWS

10'

10'

PLACE THIS EDGE OF APPLE EVEN WITH EDGE OF 1×6

CENTER MIDDLE SHELF SUPPORTS ON THE CENTER 1×6 ON THE SIDES

SHELF SUPPORT ASSEMBLY

9 With the upper shelves in position, attach the roof frame to the front panel and back panel with 1¼" screws as shown. ROOF FRAME PART A is attached to the interior side of the pencils. ROOF FRAME PART B is attached to the exterior side of ROOF FRAME PART A.

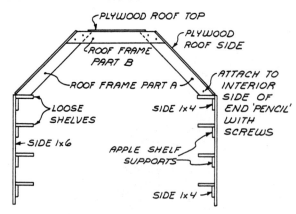

CROSS-SECTION SHOWING ROOF ASSEMBLY

10 Using paint or waterproof markers, add lines and circles to the two painted roof sides as shown to resemble notebook paper. Attach all three plywood pieces to the roof frame as shown in the ROOF ASSEMBLY CROSS-SECTION, using ¾ × 6 screws. The edges of the plywood roof top will be flush with the outer edge of ROOF FRAME PART B. The edges of the plywood roof sides will extend ¾" on both sides beyond the outer edge of ROOF FRAME PART A.

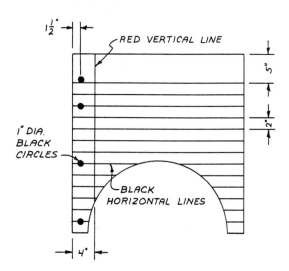

LINE GUIDE FOR ROOF SIDES

11 Cut one RACE TRACK SUPPORT as shown. Sand. Paint red.

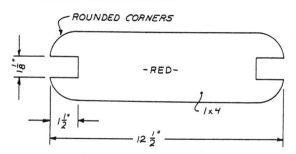

RACE TRACK SUPPORT

12 Nail moulding strips on 1 × 2s as shown. Paint exterior surfaces red, leaving track unpainted (for indoor use). Place track support piece in a window and add tracks.

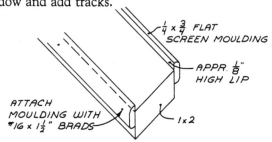

RACETRACK

Note: A great use for the leftover scraps of wood is a homemade building block set. Sand the pieces smooth and paint with whatever colors you have left.

APA THREE-STAGE CABIN

Courtesy of American Plywood Association
Tacoma, Washington
Architects: Buff, Straub & Hensman, Los Angeles, California

This multi-use structure grows with your needs; it can be built in stages as time and money permit. Although the cabin is designed for warmer times of year, it can be winterized with insulation all around.

The basic unit consists of an 8′ × 24′ enclosed area for play or storage or both, and an 8′ × 24′ shaded wood deck. Imagine the possibilities: space where your children can exercise their imaginations, bodies, and lungs! If you're into Scouting or other youth groups, this makes an ideal meeting place. During the winter season, the enclosed area provides ample storage space for lawn furniture, bicycles, and gardening equipment. No plumbing or wiring is included in this stage.

The second stage extends the deck to provide a 12′ × 24′ screened porch for bug-free outdoor relaxation and fun. Kitchen and bathroom conveniences can be added to increase the usefulness of the cabin.

What a great place for family get-togethers as your immediate family and extended family grow.

During the final construction stage the cabin becomes a small but complete house with a fully functioning kitchen and bathroom, a bedroom, and a prefab fireplace in the living room. Again, imagine the possibilities: the first home for a grown child; an office or a workshop for you or your spouse's home-based business; rental property for extra income; a guest cottage or living quarters for a caretaker.

NOTES

1 These plans were first published in 1959 and have not been updated. The builder is responsible for making sure the cabin, as constructed, meets all building code requirements.

2 DFPA (Douglas Fir Plywood Association) is now the American Plywood Association (APA).

FOUNDATION	CONCRETE
FORMWORK	SONAIRDUCT OR PAPER FORMS
FRAMING	SELECT STRUCTURAL, CONSTRUCTION & STANDARD GRADE FIR AS NOTED
PLYWOOD—ROOF	1/2" INT-DFPA • A-D (1)
PLYWOOD—WALLS	3/4" EXT-DFPA • A-C (1)
PLYWOOD—PARTITION	3/8" INT-DFPA • A-D (1)
PLYWOOD—CABINETS	3/4" INT-DFPA • A-D
PLYWOOD—UNDERLAYMENT	1/4" INT-DFPA • A-D (2)
WINDOW AND DOOR STOPS	VERTICAL GRAIN DOUGLAS FIR (3)
EXPOSED WOODWORK & DECK	TREAT WITH WATER REPELLANT
WINDOW SCREENS & DOORS	PLASTIC SCREEN IN DOUBLE 1" x 2" FRAMES
GLASS PANEL DOORS	VERTICAL GRAIN DOUGLAS FIR (3)
GLASS	1/8" DSB AND 3/16" CRYSTAL AS NOTED
MEDICINE CABINET & BATH ACCESS.	M.C. 16" x 24" WITH MIRROR - OWNER'S SELECTION
DOOR & CABINET HARDWARE	BRASS OR ALUMINUM WITH DULL CHROME FINISH
KITCHEN & BATH COUNTERS	HEAVY GAUGE (1/8") LINOLEUM (4)
SLIDING PANELS (STORAGE CABINET)	1/4" PERFORATED TEMPERED HARDBOARD (5)
BACK PANELS (STORAGE CABINET)	1/8" PERFORATED TEMPERED HARDBOARD (5)
METAL SHOWER	WITH PRECAST TERRAZZO SHOWER FLOOR
WATER CLOSET	VITREOUS CHINA
LAVATORY	ENAMELED CAST IRON
KITCHEN SINK	ENAMELED CAST IRON
SINK & SHOWER TRIM	BRASS—POLISHED CHROME FINISH
HOT WATER HEATER	40 GALLON CAPACITY
FOLDING WOOD DOOR—TO H.W.H.	WOOD & FINISH—OWNER'S SELECTION
SURFACE BURNER TOP	STAINLESS STEEL TOP 21" x 23"
RANGE HOOD	STAINLESS STEEL WITH FAN & LIGHT
REFRIGERATOR	UNDER COUNTER TYPE (4 CU. FT.)
FIREPLACE	MANCHESTER PIERCE SHEET STEEL OR EQUAL
FLUE	GLASS WOOL INSULATED GALVANIZED IRON
LIGHTING FIXTURES	OWNER'S SELECTION
WOOD FINISHING	
WOOD FRAMEWORK & TRIM	2 COATS STAIN—OWNER'S SELECTION
EXTERIOR FIR PLYWOOD WALLS	PRIMER—2 COATS HOUSE PAINT
INTERIOR FIR PLYWOOD WALLS	PRIMER—2 COATS FLAT ENAMEL
FIR PLYWOOD CABINETS	PRIMER—2 COATS SEMI-GLOSS ENAMEL
WOOD DECK	2 COATS STAIN OR PRIMER & 2 COATS PORCH ENAMEL
FLOOR (OWNER'S SELECTION)	ASPHALT OR VINYL TILE

NOTES:

(1) For plywood with excellent face appearance for paint, USE MEDIUM DENSITY EXTERIOR FIR PLYWOOD.

(2) UNDERLAYMENT STRUC.-INT C^{REP}D may be substituted for INT-DFPA • A-D or use EXT-DFPA UNDERLAYMENT if unusual moisture conditions exist.

(3) Substitute wood of comparable grade, if vertical grain Douglas fir is unavailable.

(4) Counter tops may be 3/4" HIGH DENSITY EXTERIOR FIR PLYWOOD or formica.

(5) To eliminate finishing and reduce maintenance, use plastic-faced hardboard.

FIRST STAGE CONSTRUCTION

USE				NO. & SIZE	LIN. OR SQ. FT.	BD. FT.	REMARKS
FOUNDATION	Cement			3 3/4 sacks			
	Gravel			1/2 cu. yd.			
	Sand			3/8 cu. yd.			
	Sonairduct			8 @ 10" diam.	48" long		
	Steel anchor bolts			4 @ 1/2" diam.	16" long		
	Steel anchor bolts			4 @ 1/2" diam.	20" long		
WOOD FRAMING	BUILT-UP BEAMS • 2" X 12"						
Select Structural	FLOOR			1 @ 16'0"	16		
Douglas Fir				8 @ 20'0"	160		
	ROOF			8 @ 8'0"	64		
				8 @ 18'0"	148		
					388	776	
Construction Grade	FLOOR	Blocking	2" x 6"	15 @ 8'0"	120		
			4" x 12"	2 @ 8'0"	16		
			4" x 6"	1 @ 4'0"	4		
		Decking	2" x 6"	43 @ 8'0"	344		
			2" x 6"	33 @ 16'0"	528		
	ROOF	Blocking	2" x 4"	11 @ 8'0"	88		
		Purlins	4" x 4"	36 @ 8'0"	288		
		Blocking	4" x 6"	4 @ 20'0"	80		
		Facia	2" x 6"	8 @ 12'0"	96		
					1564	1763	
WALL FRAMING							
	Posts		4" x 4"	13 @ 8'0"	104		
			4" x 4"	4 @ 10'0"	40		
	Wall plates		2" x 4"	13 @ 8'0"	104		
	Door heads		2" x 4"	3 @ 8'0"	24		
	Window mullions		2" x 4"	1 @ 6'0"	6		
					278	341	
MISCELLANEOUS LUMBER	Head & sill @ sliding panels		2" x 3"	6 @ 8'0"	48		
			3/4" x 1"	3 @ 8'0"	24		
			1 1/8" x 2 5/8"	3 @ 8'0"	24		
Construction Grade	Fixed window & door stops	1/2" x 1 1/2"		21 @ 8'0"	168		
Douglas Fir	Wall battens		1" x 4"	13 @ 8'0"	104		
	Filler		1" x 2"	2 @ 8'0"	16		
	Stair stringers		2" x 10"	3 @ 6'0"	18		
					402		
FIR PLYWOOD	Wall Panels • EXT-DFPA • A-C			11 @ 3/4" x 4'0" x 8'0"	352		
Exterior & Interior	Roof • INT-DFPA • A-D			17 @ 1/2" x 4'0" x 8'0"	544		
MISCELLANEOUS	Doors			6 @ 1 3/8" x 2'6" x 6'8"			
				3 @ 1 3/8" x 2'8" x 6'8"			
	Glass			1/8" DSB	42		
	Sliding panels	• 3/4" metal track		3 @ 4'0"	12		
		• 3/4" x 3/4" aluminum		3 @ 8'0"	24		
		• pulls		6 each			US - 26D finish
	Metal flashing			26 ga. galv. iron	80		See drawings
	Gravel stop			26 ga. galv. iron	94		As required
	Door butts			5 pr. 3 1/2" x 3 1/2"			US - 26D finish
	Head & foot surface bolts			3 pr. 3/8" x 3"			US - 26D finish
	Lock sets			3 ea. owner's selection			US - 26D finish
	Nails, bolts & washers for framing			See drawings			Non-corrosive
	Weatherstripping			3/8" wood pile	3		Sliding panels
	Paint, stain & finishing materials			Owner's selection			As required
	Built-up roofing materials			5.3 sq.			

SECOND STAGE CONSTRUCTION

SAME AS FIRST STAGE CONSTRUCTION BUT ADD THE FOLLOWING:

	USE	NO. & SIZE	LIN. OR SQ. FT.	BD. FT.	REMARKS
Standard Grade	WALL FRAMING				
Douglas Fir	Wall studs, plates & blocking • 2" x 4"	11 @ 8'0"	88	59	
FIR PLYWOOD	Wardrobe • INT-DFPA • A-D	5 @ 3/4 x 4'0" x 8'0"	160		
Interior Type	Sliding Doors • INT-DFPA • A-D	2 @ 1/4 x 4'0" x 8'0"	64		
Kitchen & bath cabinets • INT-DFPA • A-D		6 @ 3/4 x 4'0" x 8'0"	192		
		2 @ 1/4 x 4'0" x 8'0"	64		
Interior partition • INT-DFPA • A-D		4 @ 3/8 x 4'0" x 8'0"	128		
Underlayment • INT-DFPA • A-D		6 @ 1/4 x 4'0" x 8'0"	192		
			888		
PLUMBING AND ELECTRICAL EQUIPMENT	Under counter refrigerator, surface top burners, hood & duct work & sink				Owner's selection
	Metal shower	32" x 32" terrazzo floor			Owner's selection
	Hot water heater	40 gal. electric			Owner's selection
	Lavatory, medicine cab. & bath accessories				Owner's selection
	Bath wall heater	750 watt wall mounted			Owner's selection
	Lighting fixtures	See drawings			Owner's selection
MISCELLANEOUS	Wardrobe • door stiffeners	14 @ 1/2" x 1 5/8" x 8'0"	112		V.G. Fir
	• door pulls	2 @ 3/4" x 1 1/8" x 8'0"	16		V.G. Fir
	• guides	2 @ 1/4" x 1/2" x 8'0"	16		V.G. Fir
		2 @ 1/2" x 1/2" x 8'0"	16		V.G. Fir
	• facia	1 @ 3/4" x 1 5/8" x 8'0"	8		V.G. Fir
		1 @ 3/4" x 2 5/8" x 8'0"	8		V.G. Fir
	• jamb	1 @ 3/4" x 5 1/2" x 8'0"	8		V.G. Fir
	Folding wood door (HWH)	3'0" x 6'8"			Owner's selection
	Wardrobe pole & escutcheons	1 3/8" diam. 8'0" long			V.G. Douglas Fir
FINISH HARDWARE (Kitchen & Bath)	Cabinet Hinges	20 ea. owner's selection			US-26D finish
	Cabinet & drawer pulls	15 ea. owner's selection			US-26D finish
	Cabinet door catches	11 ea. owner's selection			

THIRD STAGE CONSTRUCTION

DELETE REMOVABLE SCREENS & DOORS WITH FINISH HARDWARE — OTHERWISE INCLUDE ALL MATERIALS OF PRECEDING STAGES BUT ADD THE FOLLOWING:

	USE		NO. & SIZE	LIN. OR SQ. FT.	BD. FT.	REMARKS
FIR PLYWOOD	Wall panels	● EXT-DFPA ● A-C	1 @ 3/8" x 4'0" x 4'0"	16		
Exterior & Interior	Wall panels	● EXT-DFPA ● A-C	6 @ 3/4" x 4'0" x 8'0"	192		
	Underlayment	● INT-DFPA ● A-D	9 @ 1/4" x 4'0" x 8'0"	288		
	Storage Cabinet	● INT-DFPA ● A-D	1 @ 3/4" x 4'0" x 8'0"	32		
PERFORATED HARDBOARD	Storage cabinet		1 @ 1/8" x 4'0" x 4'0"	16		
	Storage cabinet	● sliding doors	1 @ 1/4" x 2'0" x 2'0"	4		
MISCELLANEOUS LUMBER	Wall battens	1" x 4"	8 @ 8'0"	64		Construction Grade
Douglas Fir	Mullion plates	1" x 8"	2 @ 6'0"	12		Construction Grade
Fixed window & door stops		1" x 2"	9 @ 6'0"	54		Vertical grain
			47 @ 8'0"	376		Vertical grain
MISCELLANEOUS	Glass panel doors		2 @ 1 3/4" x 3'9 1/4" x 7'4"			
	Door butts		3 pr. 4" x 4" owner's selection			US—26D finish
	Head & foot bolts		1 pr. 3/8" x 3" owner's selection			US—26D finish
	Locksets		1 ea owner's selection			US—26D finish
	Threshold		5/8" x 3 5/8" x 8'0"			Oak
	Glass (doors & transom sash incl.)		1/8" DSB	23		
			3/16" crystal sheet	204		
	Transom sash		2 ea. @ 3'0" x 3'7"	(Verify)		Shop fabricated
	Transom sash hinges		2 pr. 2" x 2"	Owner's		US—26D finish
	Transom sash catches		1 ea. 1" x 1 3/4"	selection		US—26D finish
	Nails, waterproof glue & caulking		As required			
	Paint, stain & finishing materials		Owner's selection			
	Cloth panel for speaker enclosure		3/4" x 3/4" frame	2		Stopped-in
	Canvas awning, roller & gear		See drawings			Optional
	Canvas awning roller guides		6 @ 3/4" x 1 1/4' x 8'0" channel			Optional
	Metal fireplace & smokepipe		Owner's selection			Manchester Pierce or equal
	Firebrick		As required			
	Washed river stone base & mortar		As required			See drawings
	Tile flooring		9" x 9"	482		Owner's selection
	Additional lighting fixtures		As required			Owner's selection
	Septic tank, piping & drain field		As required			Per local code

THIRD STAGE CONSTRUCTION (ALTERNATE)

SAME AS FIRST AND SECOND STAGE CONSTRUCTION BUT ADD THE FOLLOWING:

	USE		NO. & SIZE	LIN. OR SQ. FT.	BD. FT.	REMARKS
FOUNDATION	Cement		1 1/4 sacks			
	Gravel		1/4 cu. yd.			
	Sand		1/8 cu. yd.			
	Sonairduct		3 @ 10" diam.	48" long		
	Steel anchor bolts		3 @ 1/2" diam.	20" long		
	Stair foundation		3 • 9" conc. pier blocks			Pre-cast
WOOD FRAMING	BUILT-UP BEAMS	2" X 12"				
Select Structural Douglas Fir	DECK		6 @ 20'0"	120	240	
Construction Grade Douglas Fir	FLOOR blocking	2" x 6"	17 @ 8'0"	136		
		4" x 12"	2 @ 6'0"	12		
	Decking	2" x 6"	17 @ 8'0"	136		
	Deck • end blocking	2" x 2"	46 @ 16'0"	736		
	Floor plates	2" x 4"	5 @ 8'0"	40		
	Deck seat & back	2" x 4"	7 @ 18'0"	126		
	Deck railing	2" x 4"	4 @ 16'0"	64		
	Seat support	2" x 4"	1 @ 10'0"	10		
	Deck railing (top)	2" x 6"	1 @ 18'0"	18		
				1318	1214	
	VERTICAL FRAMEWORK					
	Posts	4" x 6"	4 @ 14'0"	56		
	Railing posts	4" x 4"	3 @ 4'0"	12		
				68	128	
	Window & screen mullions		6 @ 8'0"	48		
	& muntins	2 " 4"	5 @ 12'0"	60		
				108	72	
	Removable screens	1" x 2"	91 @ 8'0"	728		
	Screen doors	1" x 2"	12 @ 8'0"	96		
				824		
FINISH HARDWARE	SCREEN HARDWARE					
	Transom catches		56 @ 1" x 1 3/4" spring loaded			US-26D finish
	Screen door hinges		3 pr. 3 1/2" x 3 1/2"			US-26D finish
	Screen door latch		1 only owner's selection			US-26D finish
	Screen door head & foot bolts		1 pr. 3/8" x 3" owner's selection			US-26D finish
MISCELLANEOUS	Nails, bolts & washers for framing					
	Paint, stain & finishing materials		Owner selection			As required

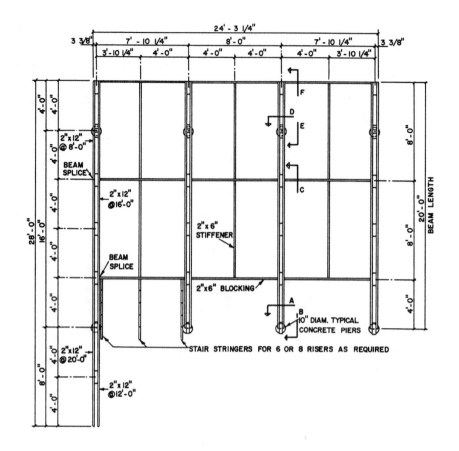

FLOOR FRAMING PLAN - 1st AND 2nd STAGE

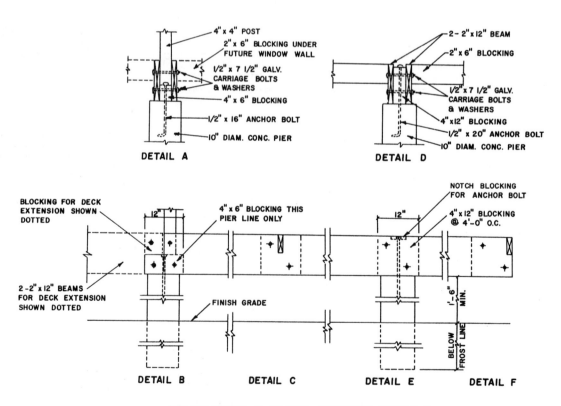

FOUNDATION & FLOOR FRAMING DETAILS

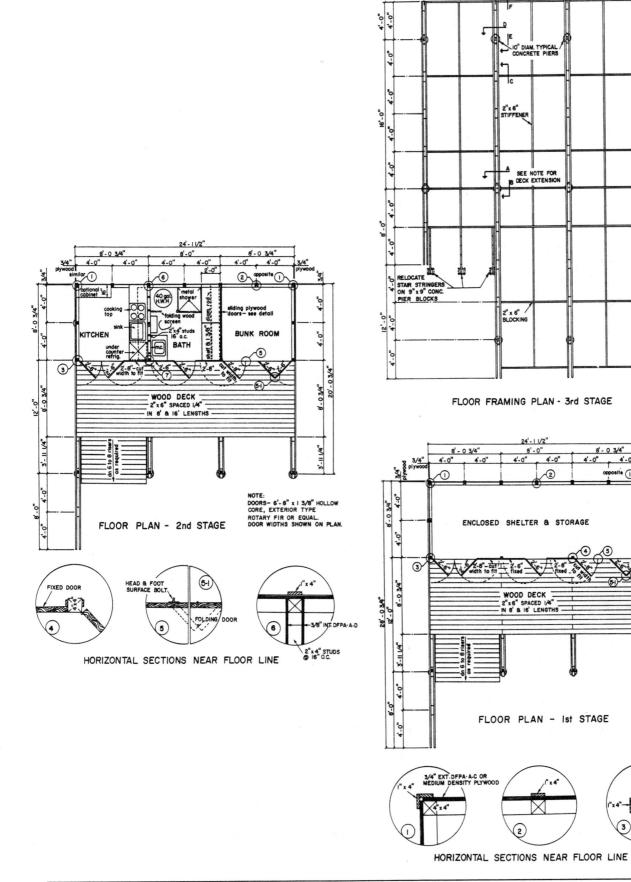

FLOOR FRAMING PLAN - 3rd STAGE

10" DIAM. TYPICAL
CONCRETE PIERS

2" x 6" STIFFENER

SEE NOTE FOR
DECK EXTENSION

RELOCATE
STAIR STRINGERS
ON 9" x 9" CONC.
PIER BLOCKS

2" x 6" BLOCKING

FLOOR PLAN - 2nd STAGE

optional cabinet

cooking top

sink

under counter refrig.

KITCHEN

40 gal. H.W.H

folding wood screen

2" x 6" studs 16" o.c.

BATH

metal shower

shelf

sliding plywood doors - see detail

BUNK ROOM

WOOD DECK
2" x 6" SPACED 1/4"
IN 8' & 16' LENGTHS

dn 6 to 8 risers as required

NOTE:
DOORS - 6'-8" x 1 3/8" HOLLOW
CORE, EXTERIOR TYPE
ROTARY FIR OR EQUAL.
DOOR WIDTHS SHOWN ON PLAN.

FIXED DOOR

4

HEAD & FOOT
SURFACE BOLT

5

5-1

FOLDING DOOR

1" x 4"

6

3/8" INT. DFPA - A-D

2" x 4" STUDS @ 16" O.C.

HORIZONTAL SECTIONS NEAR FLOOR LINE

ENCLOSED SHELTER & STORAGE

WOOD DECK
2" x 6" SPACED 1/4"
IN 8' & 16' LENGTHS

dn 6 to 8 risers as required

FLOOR PLAN - 1st STAGE

3/4" EXT. DFPA - A-C OR
MEDIUM DENSITY PLYWOOD

1" x 4"

4" x 4"

1

1" x 4"

2

1" x 4"

1" x 2"

3

HORIZONTAL SECTIONS NEAR FLOOR LINE

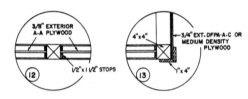

HORIZONTAL SECTIONS NEAR FLOOR LINE

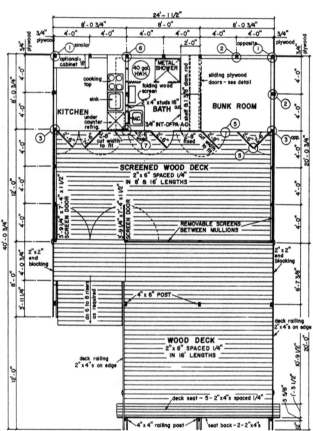

FLOOR PLAN- 3rd STAGE (ALTERNATE)

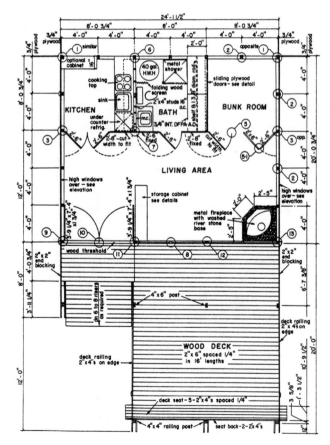

FLOOR PLAN - 3rd STAGE

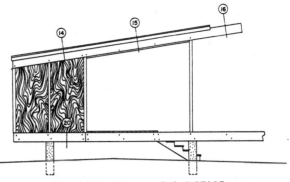

LEFT ELEVATION - 1st & 2nd STAGE

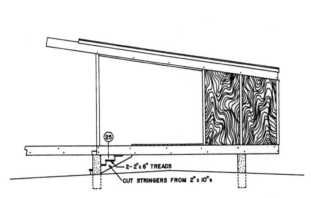

RIGHT ELEVATION - 1st & 2nd STAGE

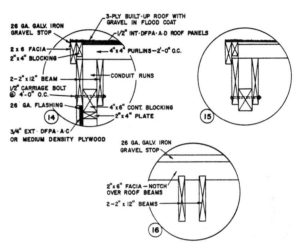

3-PLY BUILT-UP ROOF WITH GRAVEL IN FLOOD COAT
1/2" INT-DFPA-A-D ROOF PANELS
26 GA. GALV. IRON GRAVEL STOP
2 x 6 FACIA
2"x 4" BLOCKING
4"x4" PURLINS-2'-0" O.C.
2-2"x12" BEAM
CONDUIT RUNS
1/2" CARRIAGE BOLT @ 4'-0" O.C.
26 GA. FLASHING
4"x 6" CONT. BLOCKING
2"x4" PLATE
3/4" EXT. DFPA-A-C OR MEDIUM DENSITY PLYWOOD

26 GA. GALV. IRON GRAVEL STOP
2"x 6" FACIA — NOTCH OVER ROOF BEAMS
2-2"x 12" BEAMS

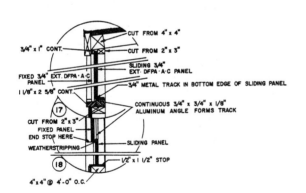

CUT FROM 4"x 4"
3/4"x 1" CONT.
CUT FROM 2"x 3"
SLIDING 3/4" EXT. DFPA-A-C PANEL
FIXED 3/4" EXT. DFPA-A-C PANEL
3/4" METAL TRACK IN BOTTOM EDGE OF SLIDING PANEL
1 1/8" x 2 5/8" CONT.
CONTINUOUS 3/4" x 3/4" x 1/8" ALUMINUM ANGLE FORMS TRACK
CUT FROM 2"x 3"
FIXED PANEL END STOP HERE
WEATHERSTRIPPING
SLIDING PANEL
1/2" x 1 1/2" STOP
4"x 4" @ 4'-0" O.C.

2-2"x 6" TREADS
CUT STRINGERS FROM 2"x 10"s

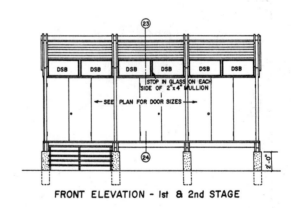

DSB DSB DSB DSB DSB DSB
STOP IN GLASS ON EACH SIDE OF 2"x 4" MULLION
SEE PLAN FOR DOOR SIZES

FRONT ELEVATION - 1st & 2nd STAGE

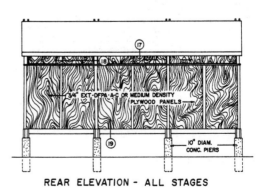

3/4" EXT-DFPA-A-C OR MEDIUM DENSITY PLYWOOD PANELS
10" DIAM. CONC. PIERS

REAR ELEVATION - ALL STAGES

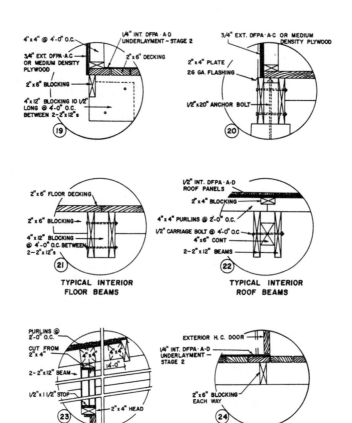

TYPICAL INTERIOR
FLOOR BEAMS

TYPICAL INTERIOR
ROOF BEAMS

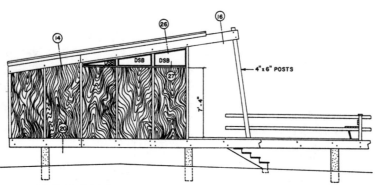

LEFT ELEVATION – 3rd STAGE – RIGHT ELEVATION SIMILAR

NOTE:
ALL GLAZING SHALL BE DSB OR CRYSTAL SHEET
AS NOTED. SET ALL STOPS AND BACK OF GLAZING
IN FULL BED OF MASTIC EXCEPT INSIDE STOPS
AT HEADS AND SILLS WHICH SHALL BE SET
WITH WATERPROOF GLUE AND FINISH NAILS.

ALL WINDOW MEMBERS SHALL BE CONSTRUCTION
GRADE FIR EXCEPT STOPS WHICH SHALL BE
V.G. FIR. USE WOOD OF EQUIVALENT GRADE
IF DOUGLAS FIR IS UNAVAILABLE.

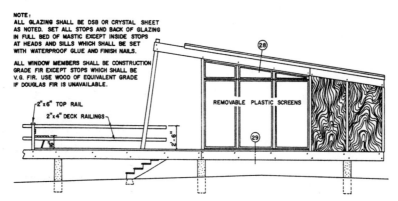

RIGHT ELEVATION – 3rd STAGE (ALTERNATE) – LEFT ELEVATION SIMILAR

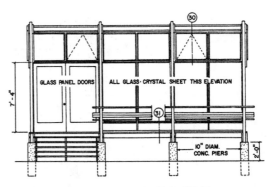

FRONT ELEVATION - 3rd STAGE

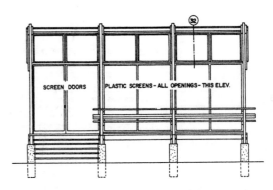

FRONT ELEVATION - 3rd STAGE (ALTERNATE)

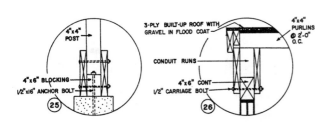

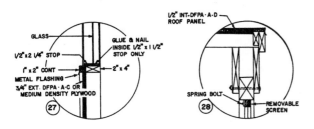

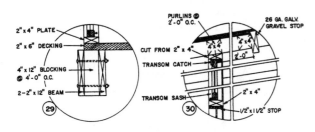

STRUCTURAL NOTES:

ROOF DESIGNED FOR 25 LBS. PER SQ. FT. MAXIMUM LIVE LOAD. FLOOR DESIGNED FOR 40 LBS. PER SQ. FT. MAXIMUM LIVE LOAD.

FLOOR & ROOF BUILT-UP BEAM MEMBERS, MINIMUM - SELECT STRUCTURAL DOUGLAS FIR (1900f).

ALL OTHER STRUCTURAL WOOD, MINIMUM – "CONSTRUCTION" GRADE DOUGLAS FIR (1500f) EXCEPT AS NOTED.

IF DOUGLAS FIR IS UNAVAILABLE CONSULT LOCAL BUILDING AUTHORITY FOR WOOD EQUIVALENT IN FIBER STRESS OR ALTERNATELY INCREASE SIZE OF STRUCTURAL MEMBERS.

CONSULT LOCAL BUILDING AUTHORITY FOR ALLOWABLE LIVE LOADS FOR FLOOR AND ROOF. IF ALLOWABLE LIVE LOADS ARE IN EXCESS OF THOSE STATED ABOVE, DUE TO SNOW, ETC., SIZE OF STRUCTURAL MEMBERS MUST BE INCREASED PROPORTIONATELY TO SUPPORT THE ADDITIONAL LOAD.

RUN ALL CONCRETE PIERS TO SOLID UNDISTURBED BEARING AND BELOW LOCAL FROST LINE.

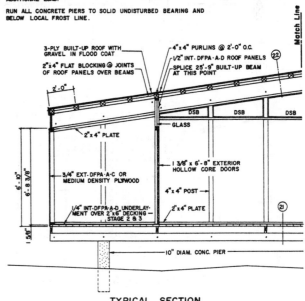

TYPICAL SECTION

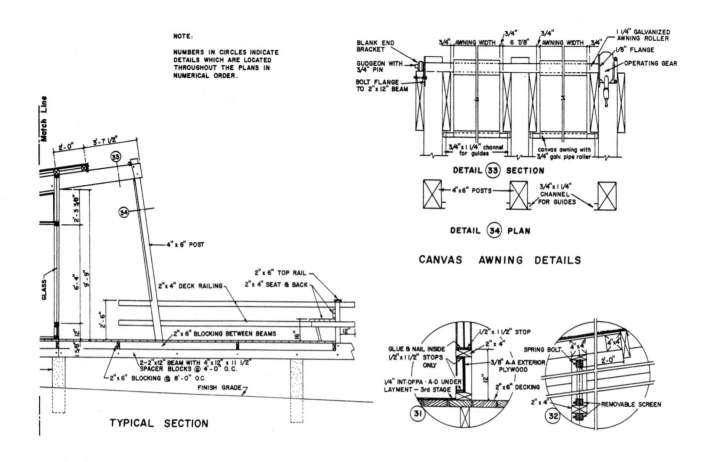

NOTE:

NUMBERS IN CIRCLES INDICATE DETAILS WHICH ARE LOCATED THROUGHOUT THE PLANS IN NUMERICAL ORDER.

TYPICAL SECTION

CANVAS AWNING DETAILS

DETAIL ③③ SECTION

DETAIL ③④ PLAN

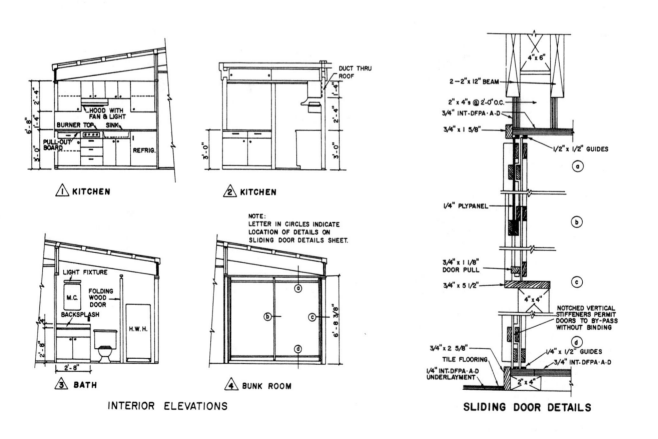

① KITCHEN

② KITCHEN

③ BATH

④ BUNK ROOM

NOTE:
LETTER IN CIRCLES INDICATE LOCATION OF DETAILS ON SLIDING DOOR DETAILS SHEET.

INTERIOR ELEVATIONS

SLIDING DOOR DETAILS

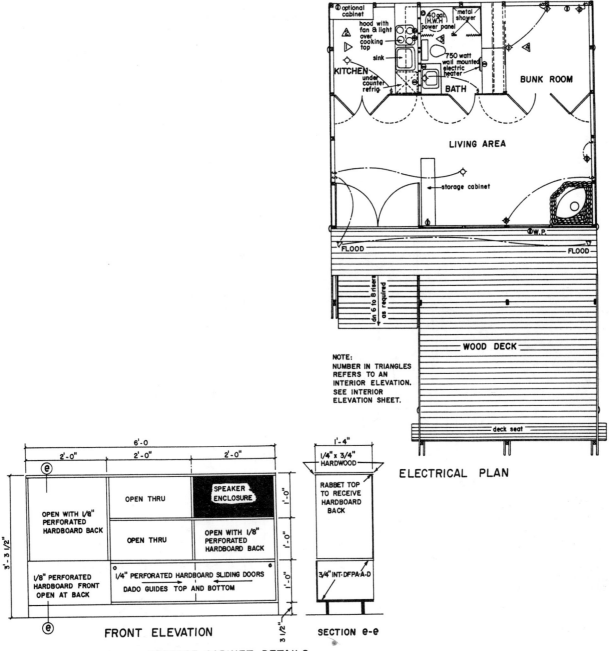

ELECTRICAL PLAN

In floor plan:
- optional cabinet
- hood with fan & light over cooking top
- sink
- KITCHEN
- under counter refrig.
- 40 gal. (H.W.H) power panel
- metal shower
- 750 watt wall mounted electric heater
- BATH
- BUNK ROOM
- LIVING AREA
- storage cabinet
- FLOOD
- FLOOD
- W.P.
- dn 6 to 8 risers as required
- WOOD DECK
- deck seat

NOTE:
NUMBER IN TRIANGLES
REFERS TO AN
INTERIOR ELEVATION.
SEE INTERIOR
ELEVATION SHEET.

STORAGE CABINET DETAILS

FRONT ELEVATION

6'-0"
2'-0" | 2'-0" | 2'-0"
3'-3 1/2"

- OPEN WITH 1/8" PERFORATED HARDBOARD BACK
- OPEN THRU
- SPEAKER ENCLOSURE
- OPEN THRU
- OPEN WITH 1/8" PERFORATED HARDBOARD BACK
- 1/8" PERFORATED HARDBOARD FRONT OPEN AT BACK
- 1/4" PERFORATED HARDBOARD SLIDING DOORS DADO GUIDES TOP AND BOTTOM
- 1'-0" (×3)
- 3 1/2"

SECTION e-e

- 1'-4"
- 1/4" x 3/4" HARDWOOD
- RABBET TOP TO RECEIVE HARDBOARD BACK
- 3/4" INT·DFPA·A·D

ELECTRICAL SYMBOLS

SYMBOL	DESCRIPTION
◇	HANGING CEILING FIXTURE CONDUIT: RUN ON TOP OF 4" x 6" IN BUILT-UP ROOF BEAM.
⊕	BRACKET LIGHT FIXTURE MOUNTED ON FACE OF BEAM OR PLATE. CONDUIT: RUN SAME AS ABOVE-THEN DRILL THRU SIDE OF BEAM.
⊖	DOUBLE CONVENIENCE OUTLET · SURFACE MOUNTED EXCEPT 2"x4" WALL. CONDUIT: RUN UNDER FLOOR TO LOCATION
$	WALL SWITCH-SURFACE MOUNTED-COVERED BOX. CONDUIT: RUN IN ROOF BEAMS WHERE PRACTICAL.
⊛	SPECIAL PURPOSE OUTLET — 220V. CONDUIT: RUN IN 2"x4" STUD WALL PER CODE.
⊖W.P.	WATERPROOF OUTLET—SURFACE MOUNTED WITH COVER. CONDUIT: RUN UNDER FLOOR.
◁	FLOODLIGHT—MOUNTED ON FACE OF ROOF BEAM. CONDUIT: RUN BETWEEN BEAMS — THEN DRILL THRU SIDE OF BEAM.

NOTE: ALL ELECTRICAL WORK PER LOCAL CODE.

BASIC SANDBOX AND DECK

Designed by Kathy Smith Anthenat

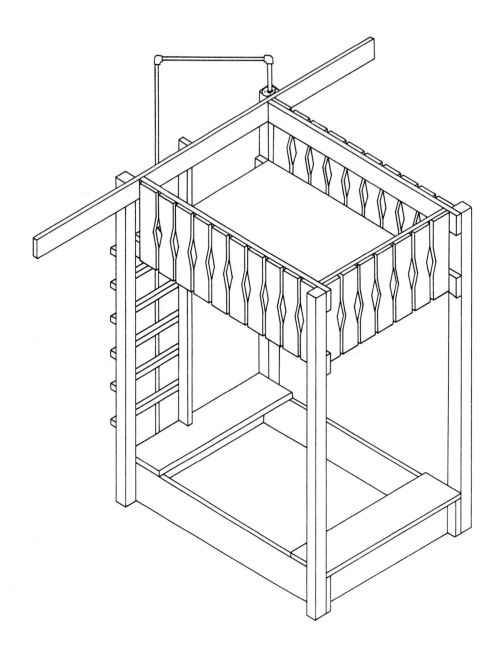

This easy to build structure minimizes frills to maximize young imaginations. The sandbox has two wide seats and is shaded by the upper deck. The deck is designed with low sides so that children can enjoy the view while sitting on the plywood floor playing games or talking. A ladder and fireman's pole are positioned together at the rear so that those who want to go up and down won't interfere with anyone who wants to sit quietly and read or play a game near the front of the deck. The decision on what to hang from the extended 2×6 has been left to you; it could be a climbing rope or net, a child's swing or baby seat, a trapeze bar or rings, or an old-time favorite—a tire.

BILL OF MATERIALS

1—4′ × 8′ sheet ¾″ exterior plywood
4—treated 4″ × 4″ × 10′
2—treated 2″ × 12″ × 6′
4—treated 2″ × 12″ × 4′
1—treated 2″ × 6″ × 10′
4—treated 2″ × 6″ × 6′
3—treated 2″ × 6″ × 4′
2—treated 2″ × 4″ × 8′
2—treated 2″ × 2″ × 6′
9—treated 1″ × 6″ × 6′
1″ galvanized pipe:
1 @ 11′-0″ long
1 @ 30″ long
1 @ 12″ long
1—1″ pipe collar
2—1″ pipe elbows
4 or 5 bags concrete mix
12—⅝″ × 5″ carriage bolts with acorn nuts
4—¼″ × 1½″ lag screws
4—½″ hex head bolts with washers, lock washer, nut
3″ plated deck screws
1½″ plated deck screws
landscape fabric

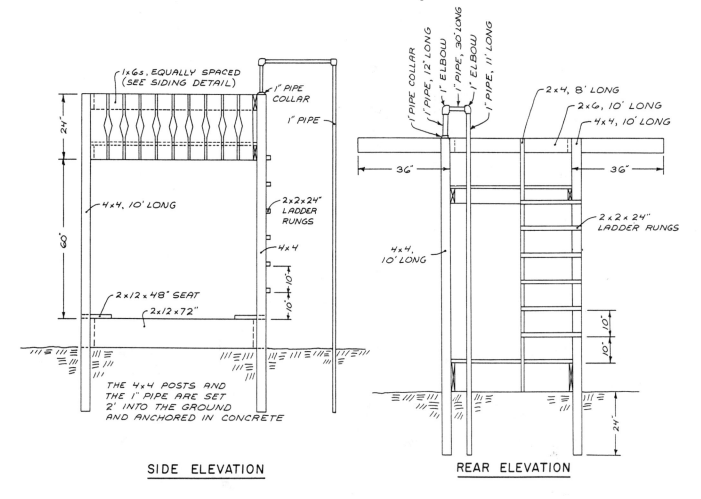

SIDE ELEVATION

REAR ELEVATION

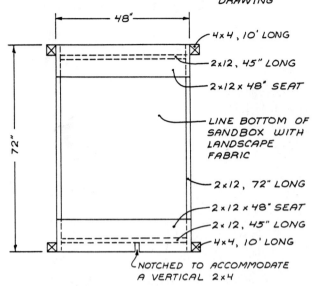

NOTE - USE 3" PLATED DECK SCREWS TO ASSEMBLE LUMBER IN THIS DRAWING

48"

72"

4x4, 10' LONG

2x12, 45" LONG

2x12 x 48" SEAT

LINE BOTTOM OF SANDBOX WITH LANDSCAPE FABRIC

2x12, 72" LONG

2x12 x 48" SEAT

2x12, 45" LONG

4x4, 10' LONG

NOTCHED TO ACCOMMODATE A VERTICAL 2x4

TOP VIEW OF SANDBOX

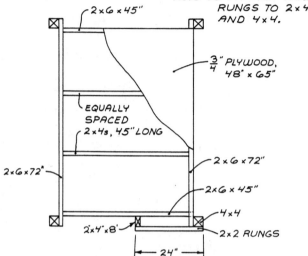

NOTE - USE 3" PLATED DECK SCREWS TO ASSEMBLE 2x6s AND 2x4s WHICH FRAME THE DECK FLOOR. USE 1½" PLATED DECK SCREWS TO ATTACH PLYWOOD TO THE FLOOR FRAME. USE ⅝" x 5" CARRIAGE BOLTS WITH ACORN NUTS TO ATTACH 2x2 RUNGS TO 2x4 AND 4x4.

2x6 x 45"

¾" PLYWOOD, 48" x 65"

EQUALLY SPACED 2x4s, 45" LONG

2x6 x 72"

2x6 x 72"

2x6 x 45"

4x4

2x4 x 8'

2x2 RUNGS

24"

TOP VIEW OF PLYWOOD DECK

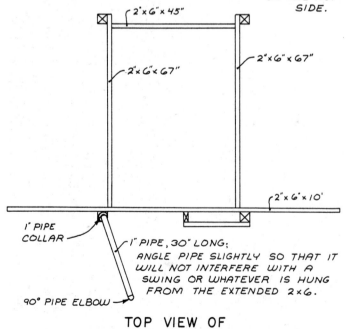

NOTE - USE ¼" x 1½" LAG SCREWS TO ATTACH PIPE COLLAR TO TOP OF 4x4 POST.
TO ATTACH 2x6 x 10' TO THE 4x4 POSTS, POSITION 2x6 AND DRILL TWO 9/16" HOLES AT EACH POST. INSERT ½" HEX HEAD BOLTS WITH WASHERS ON BOTH SIDES AND LOCK WASHERS ON THE NUT SIDE.

2"x 6" x 45"

2"x 6" x 67"

2"x 6" x 67"

2"x 6" x 10'

1" PIPE COLLAR

1" PIPE, 30" LONG; ANGLE PIPE SLIGHTLY SO THAT IT WILL NOT INTERFERE WITH A SWING OR WHATEVER IS HUNG FROM THE EXTENDED 2x6.

90° PIPE ELBOW

TOP VIEW OF
TOP RAILING

1x6

8"

4"

4"

8"

24"

1"

ATTACH SIDING TO 2x6s WITH 1½" PLATED DECK SCREWS.

THE SIDING PIECES ON EACH END ARE NOTCHED ON ONE SIDE ONLY.

THE SIDING GOES ON THREE SIDES ONLY (NOT ON THE LADDER SIDE).

SIDING DETAIL

LOFTY LOOKOUT

Designed by Thomas L. Kauffman

Children won't be the only ones wanting to play in this play house. The Lofty Lookout is equally appealing to adults and large enough to accommodate them. Imagine it in a wooded setting or overlooking a river or lake for weekend getaways.

Exterior steps lead up to a 12' by 12' room, 7' above the ground. In one corner of this room is a ladder for climbing up to the 8' by 12' loft, spacious enough for many sleeping bags. From the railing along the front edge of the loft you can see down into the room below or out the upper row of windows. The structure is about 24' high—with an abundance of windows for enjoying the view.

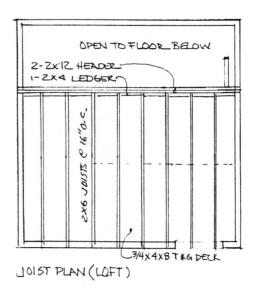

JOIST PLAN (LOFT)

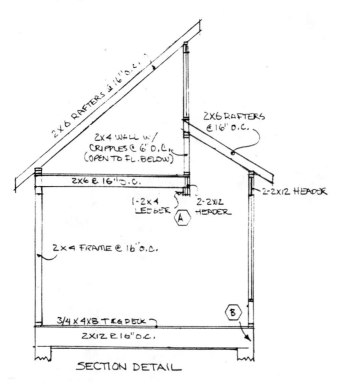

SECTION DETAIL

FOUNDATION PLAN

JOIST PLAN (MAIN LEVEL)

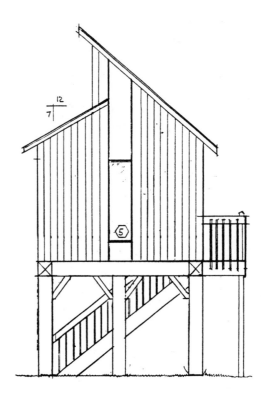

3/8" R.S. FIR PLY SOFFIT

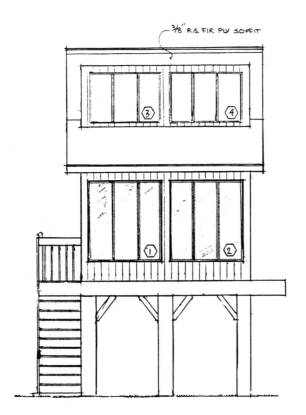

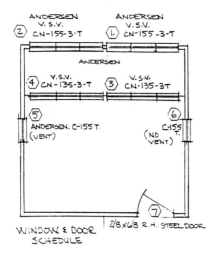

ANDERSEN
V.S.V.
② CN-155-3-T

ANDERSEN
V.S.V.
① CN-155-3-T

ANDERSEN

④ V.S.V.
CN-135-3-T

③ V.S.V.
CN-135-3T

⑤ ANDERSEN. C-155 T.
(VENT)

⑥ C-155 T.
(NO VENT)

⑦ 2/8 X 6/8 R.H. STEEL DOOR

WINDOW & DOOR
SCHEDULE

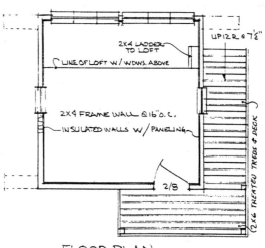

2X4 LADDER TO LOFT

LINE OF LOFT W/ WDWS. ABOVE

UP 12 R @ 7⅛"

2X4 FRAME WALL @ 16' O.C.

INSULATED WALLS W/ PANELING

2/8

(2X6 TREATED TREADS & DECK)

FLOOR PLAN

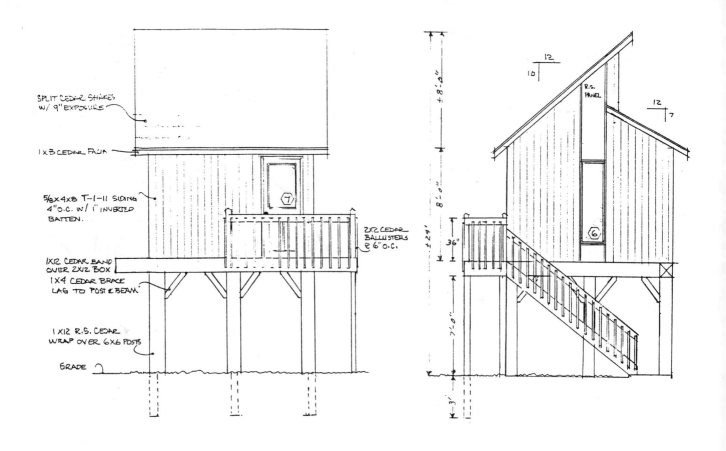

SPLIT CEDAR SHAKES
W/ 9" EXPOSURE

1 X 3 CEDAR FASIA

5/8 X 4 X 8 T-1-11 SIDING
4" O.C. W/ 1" INVERTED
BATTEN.

1 X 12 CEDAR BAND
OVER 2 X 12 BOX
1 X 4 CEDAR BRACE
LAG TO POST & BEAM

1 X 12 R.S. CEDAR
WRAP OVER 6 X 6 POSTS

GRADE

2 X 2 CEDAR
BALLUSTERS
@ 6" O.C.

12
10

± 8'-0"

R.S.
PANEL

12
7

8'-0"

± 24"

36"

7'-0"

± 3'

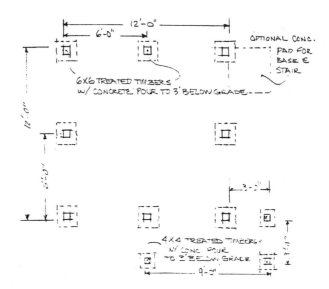

12'-0"
6'-0"

12'-0"

6'-0"

OPTIONAL CONC.
PAD FOR
BASE & STAIR

6 X 6 TREATED TIMBERS
W/ CONCRETE POUR TO 3' BELOW GRADE

3'-3"

4 X 4 TREATED TIMBERS
W/ CONC. POUR
TO 2' BELOW GRADE

9'-3"

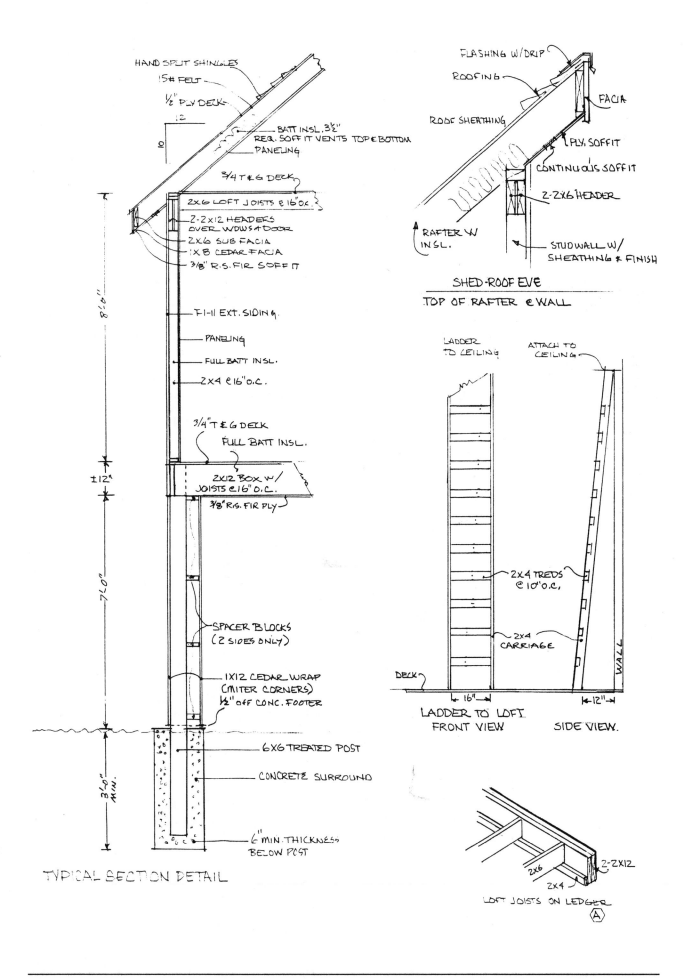

HAND SPLIT SHINGLES
15# FELT
1/2" PLY DECK
12
10
BATT INSL. 3½"
REQ. SOFFIT VENTS TOP & BOTTOM
PANELING
3/4 T&G DECK
2X6 LOFT JOISTS @ 16" O.C.
2-2X12 HEADERS OVER WDWS & DOOR
2X6 SUB FACIA
1X8 CEDAR FACIA
3/8" R.S. FIR SOFFIT

8'-0"

T-1-11 EXT. SIDING
PANELING
FULL BATT INSL.
2X4 @ 16" O.C.

3/4" T&G DECK
FULL BATT INSL.

±12"

2X12 BOX W/ JOISTS @ 16" O.C.
3/8" R.S. FIR PLY

7'-0"

SPACER BLOCKS (2 SIDES ONLY)

1X12 CEDAR WRAP (MITER CORNERS)
1/2" OFF CONC. FOOTER

6X6 TREATED POST
CONCRETE SURROUND

3'-0" MIN.

6" MIN. THICKNESS BELOW POST

TYPICAL SECTION DETAIL

FLASHING W/DRIP
ROOFING
ROOF SHEATHING
FACIA
PLY. SOFFIT
CONTINUOUS SOFFIT
2-2X6 HEADER
RAFTER W/ INSL.
STUDWALL W/ SHEATHING & FINISH

SHED-ROOF EVE
TOP OF RAFTER @ WALL

LADDER TO CEILING
ATTACH TO CEILING
2X4 TREDS @ 10" O.C.
2X4 CARRIAGE
DECK
WALL
16"
12"

LADDER TO LOFT
FRONT VIEW
SIDE VIEW

2X6
2X4
2-2X12
LOFT JOISTS ON LEDGER
Ⓐ

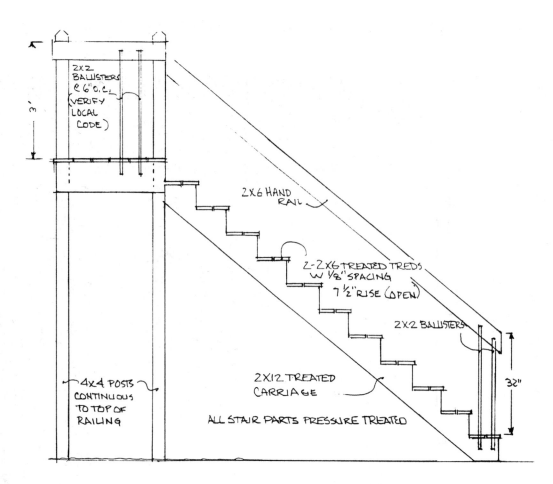

2X2
BALLISTERS
@ 6" O.C.
(VERIFY
LOCAL
CODE)

3'

2X6 HAND
RAIL

2-2X6 TREATED TREDS
W 1/8" SPACING

7 1/2" RISE (OPEN)

2X2 BALLISTERS

4X4 POSTS
CONTINUOUS
TO TOP OF
RAILING

2X12 TREATED
CARRIAGE

ALL STAIR PARTS PRESSURE TREATED

32"

STAIR & LANDING DETAIL
SCALE 1/2"=1'-0"

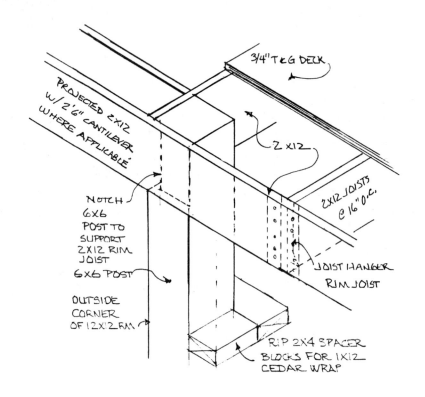

3/4" T & G DECK

PROJECTED 2X12
W/ 2'6" CANTILEVER
WHERE APPLICABLE

2 X 12

2X12 JOISTS
@ 16" O.C.

NOTCH
6X6
POST TO
SUPPORT
2X12 RIM
JOIST

6X6 POST

OUTSIDE
CORNER
OF 12X12 RM

JOIST HANGER
RIM JOIST

RIP 2X4 SPACER
BLOCKS FOR 1X12
CEDAR WRAP

BUCKEYE TRADING POST

Designed by Bruce A. Anthenat

Bring the Old West to your backyard with this adorable 6' high, frontier-style building! Reworked sections of stockade fence are used for the walls—cut and joined to imitate a log cabin at a fraction of the cost. The Buckeye Trading Post has three windows and one doorway. Leftover scraps from this project could be used to make a half-door or child-sized benches.

Construct two or more of these and you'll have a whole town for the kids to play in. The buildings could be the Sheriff's Office, Doctor's Office, Bank, Stagecoach Station, etc. The Town Square would be a large sandbox with a flagpole in the middle. Now it's time to name your frontier town!

BILL OF MATERIALS

(Treated wood is used throughout; if you cannot find the required sizes already treated, coat the wood with a preservative before assembly.)

  5 — 6' × 8' sections stockade fence (boards are ⅝" × 3¾")
  6 — 6' long ⅝" thick dog-ear fence boards (single boards)
  3 — 4' × 8' sheets ⅝" exterior plywood
  16 — 1" × 2" × 8'
  2 — 2" × 2" × 8'
  4 — 2" × 3" × 8'
  7 — 2" × 4" × 8'
  26 square feet of roofing felt
  nails

NOTES

Cut off 1½" of the bottom of the vertical boards on the side and back walls so that they will sit on top of the floor when assembled. Because the front wall sits on the porch, the bottom fence board on this wall must also be cut 1½".

Use a 2 × 4 under the roof (with ends nailed to the side walls, flush at the top) to nail the seam of the plywood roof to.

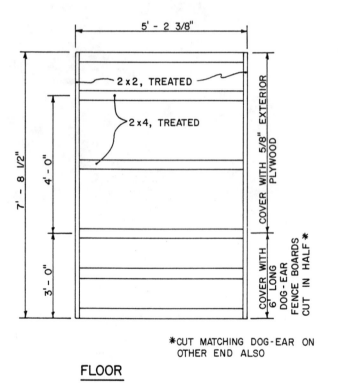

5' - 2 3/8"

7' - 8 1/2"

4' - 0"

3' - 0"

2 x 2, TREATED

2 x 4, TREATED

COVER WITH ⅝" EXTERIOR PLYWOOD

COVER WITH 6' LONG DOG-EAR FENCE BOARDS *

*CUT MATCHING DOG-EAR ON OTHER END ALSO

FLOOR

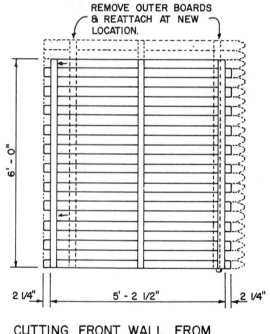

USE THESE SAME DIMENSIONS TO MAKE BACK WALL, EXCEPT THAT IT SHOULD BE 5' HIGH INSTEAD OF 6'.

REMOVE OUTER BOARDS & REATTACH AT NEW LOCATION.

6' - 0"

2 1/4"   5' - 2 1/2"   2 1/4"

CUTTING FRONT WALL FROM SECTION OF FENCE

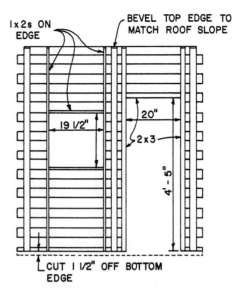

1x2s ON EDGE

BEVEL TOP EDGE TO MATCH ROOF SLOPE

19 1/2"

20"

2x3

4' - 5"

CUT 1 1/2" OFF BOTTOM EDGE

FRONT - INTERIOR VIEW

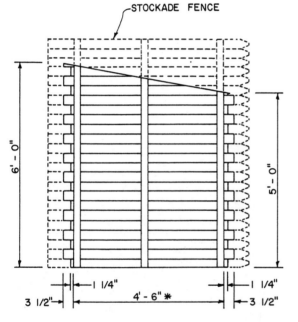

STOCKADE FENCE

6' - 0"

5' - 0"

3 1/2"   1 1/4"   4' - 6" *   1 1/4"   3 1/2"

* MAKE SURE THIS DIMENSION IS THE SAME ON BOTH SIDE PIECES.

CUTTING LEFT SIDE FROM SECTION OF FENCE

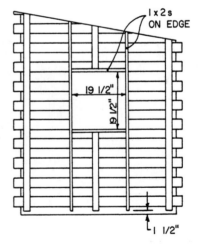

1x2s ON EDGE

19 1/2"

19 1/2"

1 1/2"

LEFT SIDE - INTERIOR VIEW

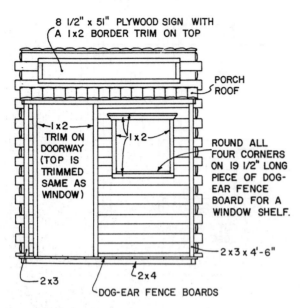

8 1/2" x 51" PLYWOOD SIGN WITH A 1x2 BORDER TRIM ON TOP

PORCH ROOF

1x2 TRIM ON DOORWAY (TOP IS TRIMMED SAME AS WINDOW)

1x2

ROUND ALL FOUR CORNERS ON 19 1/2" LONG PIECE OF DOG-EAR FENCE BOARD FOR A WINDOW SHELF.

2x3

2x4

DOG-EAR FENCE BOARDS

2 x 3 x 4'-6"

FRONT ELEVATION

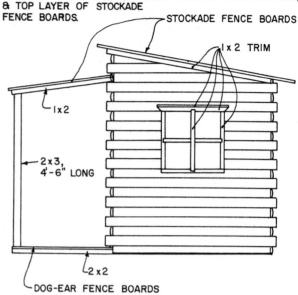

NOTE - THE ROOF OF THE CABIN CONSISTS OF A BOTTOM LAYER OF 5/8" PLYWOOD, MIDDLE LAYER OF ROOFING FELT, & TOP LAYER OF STOCKADE FENCE BOARDS.

STOCKADE FENCE BOARDS

1x2 TRIM

1x2

2x3, 4'-6" LONG

2x2

DOG-EAR FENCE BOARDS

RIGHT SIDE ELEVATION

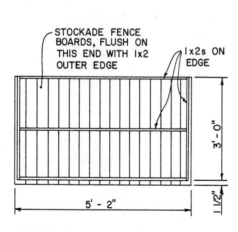

STOCKADE FENCE BOARDS, FLUSH ON THIS END WITH 1x2 OUTER EDGE

1x2s ON EDGE

3'-0"

1/2"

5'-2"

PORCH ROOF - BOTTOM VIEW

BUCKEYE TRADING POST

LETTERING FOR SIGN

1 SQUARE = 1 INCH

CAITLIN'S CASTLE

Designed by Michael Pascucci

This 8' × 8' modern-day castle will transport your child to the world of princesses and knights, moats and dragons. It includes a slide, a fireman's pole, a ship's ladder, a climbing rope, one upper deck ramp, two ground level ramps, and a separate swing set.

Flags wave from the top of the central tower and each corner of the upper deck. The shaded area below the upper deck could be filled with sand for an extra large sandbox. Caitlin's Castle can keep a whole neighborhood of kids busy for hours.

NOTES

1 Ease the edges of the posts slightly before assembly for a more finished appearance.

2 The 20′ × 10′ slide, fireman's pole, climbing rope, and swings are accessories available at larger building supply stores.

3 Add the corner flags by drilling holes for small flag poles in each corner of the 2 × 4 railing on the upper deck.

4 Lag screws and plated deck screws are used as fasteners for the castle. The locations of lag screws are indicated with large dots.

5 Use ¾″ poly rope at ramps.

6 Use pressure treated wood throughout.

Rear view of Caitlin's Castle.

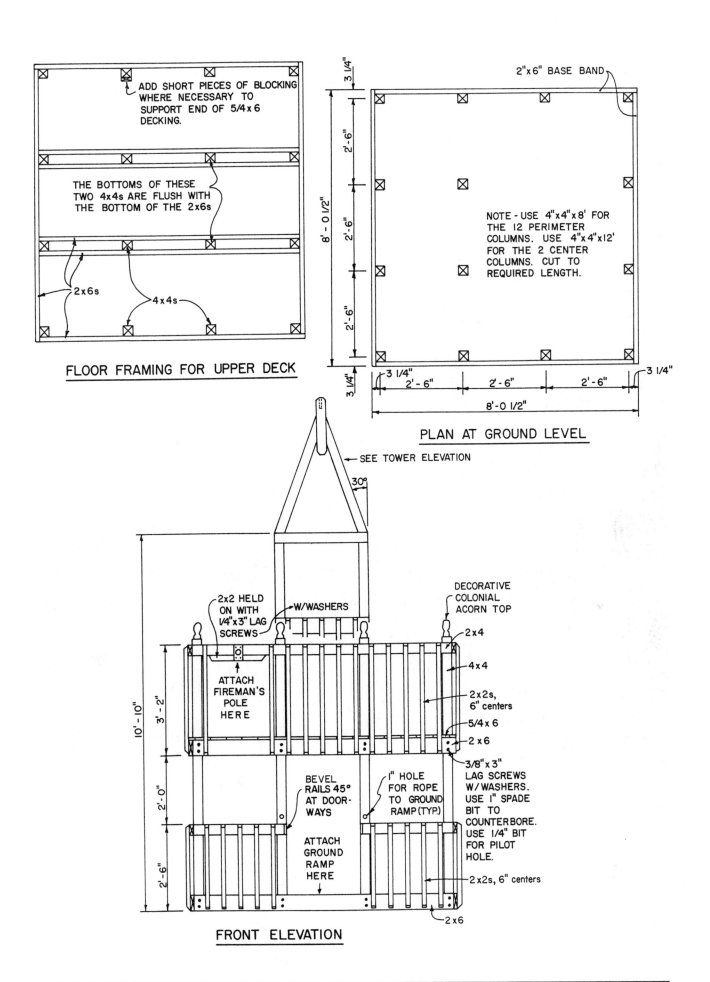

FLOOR FRAMING FOR UPPER DECK

ADD SHORT PIECES OF BLOCKING WHERE NECESSARY TO SUPPORT END OF 5/4 x 6 DECKING.

THE BOTTOMS OF THESE TWO 4x4s ARE FLUSH WITH THE BOTTOM OF THE 2x6s

2x6s

4x4s

PLAN AT GROUND LEVEL

2"x6" BASE BAND

3 1/4"

2'-6"

2'-6"

8'-0 1/2"

2'-6"

3 1/4"

NOTE - USE 4"x4"x8' FOR THE 12 PERIMETER COLUMNS. USE 4"x4"x12' FOR THE 2 CENTER COLUMNS. CUT TO REQUIRED LENGTH.

3 1/4"   2'-6"   2'-6"   2'-6"   3 1/4"

8'-0 1/2"

FRONT ELEVATION

SEE TOWER ELEVATION

30°

2x2 HELD ON WITH 1/4"x3" LAG SCREWS

W/WASHERS

DECORATIVE COLONIAL ACORN TOP

2x4

4x4

2x2s, 6" centers

5/4 x 6

2x6

ATTACH FIREMAN'S POLE HERE

10'-10"

3'-2"

2'-0"

2'-6"

BEVEL RAILS 45° AT DOOR-WAYS

ATTACH GROUND RAMP HERE

1" HOLE FOR ROPE TO GROUND RAMP (TYP.)

3/8"x3" LAG SCREWS W/WASHERS. USE 1" SPADE BIT TO COUNTERBORE. USE 1/4" BIT FOR PILOT HOLE.

2x2s, 6" centers

2x6

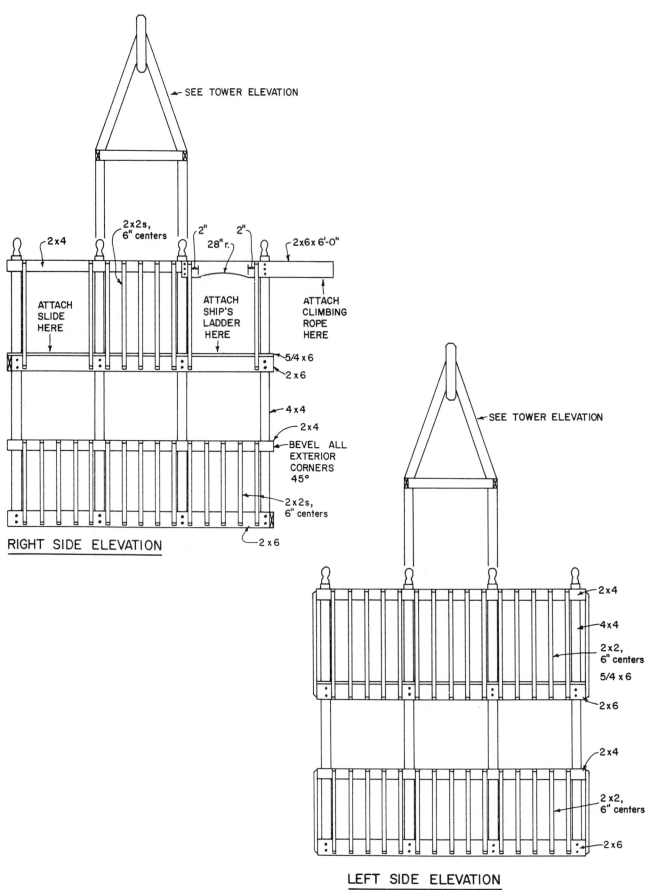

SEE TOWER ELEVATION

2x4

2x2s,
6" centers

2"

28" r.

2"

2x6x 6'-0"

ATTACH
SLIDE
HERE

ATTACH
SHIP'S
LADDER
HERE

ATTACH
CLIMBING
ROPE
HERE

5/4 x 6

2 x 6

4 x 4

2 x 4

BEVEL ALL
EXTERIOR
CORNERS
45°

2 x 2s,
6" centers

2 x 6

RIGHT SIDE ELEVATION

SEE TOWER ELEVATION

2x4

4x4

2x2,
6" centers

5/4 x 6

2x6

2x4

2x2,
6" centers

2x6

LEFT SIDE ELEVATION

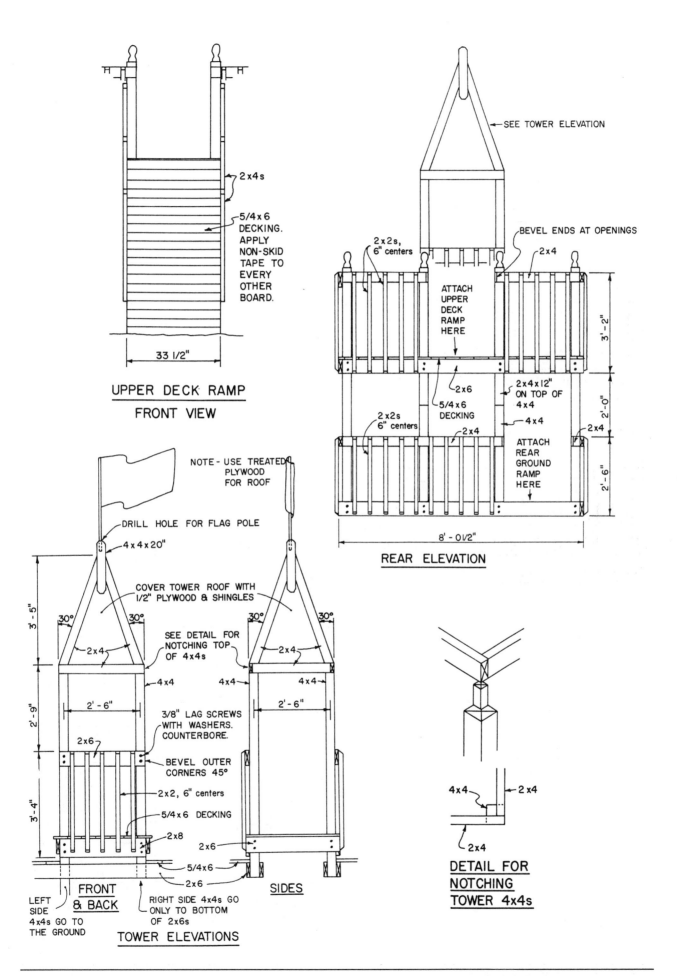

2 x 4s

5/4 x 6 DECKING. APPLY NON-SKID TAPE TO EVERY OTHER BOARD.

33 1/2"

UPPER DECK RAMP
FRONT VIEW

SEE TOWER ELEVATION

2 x 2s, 6" centers

BEVEL ENDS AT OPENINGS

2 x 4

ATTACH UPPER DECK RAMP HERE

3'-2"

2 x 6

5/4 x 6 DECKING

2 x 4 x 12" ON TOP OF 4 x 4

2'-0"

4 x 4

2 x 4

2 x 2s 6" centers

2 x 4

ATTACH REAR GROUND RAMP HERE

2'-6"

8'-0 1/2"

REAR ELEVATION

NOTE - USE TREATED PLYWOOD FOR ROOF

DRILL HOLE FOR FLAG POLE

4 x 4 x 20"

COVER TOWER ROOF WITH 1/2" PLYWOOD & SHINGLES

3'-5"

30°   30°   30°   30°

2 x 4   2 x 4

SEE DETAIL FOR NOTCHING TOP OF 4x4s

4 x 4   4 x 4   4 x 4

2'-9"

2'-6"   2'-6"

3/8" LAG SCREWS WITH WASHERS. COUNTERBORE.

2 x 6

BEVEL OUTER CORNERS 45°

2 x 2, 6" centers

3'-4"

5/4 x 6 DECKING

2 x 8

2 x 6

5/4 x 6

2 x 6

LEFT SIDE 4x4s GO TO THE GROUND

FRONT & BACK

RIGHT SIDE 4x4s GO ONLY TO BOTTOM OF 2x6s

SIDES

TOWER ELEVATIONS

4x4   2 x 4

4 x 4

DETAIL FOR NOTCHING TOWER 4x4s

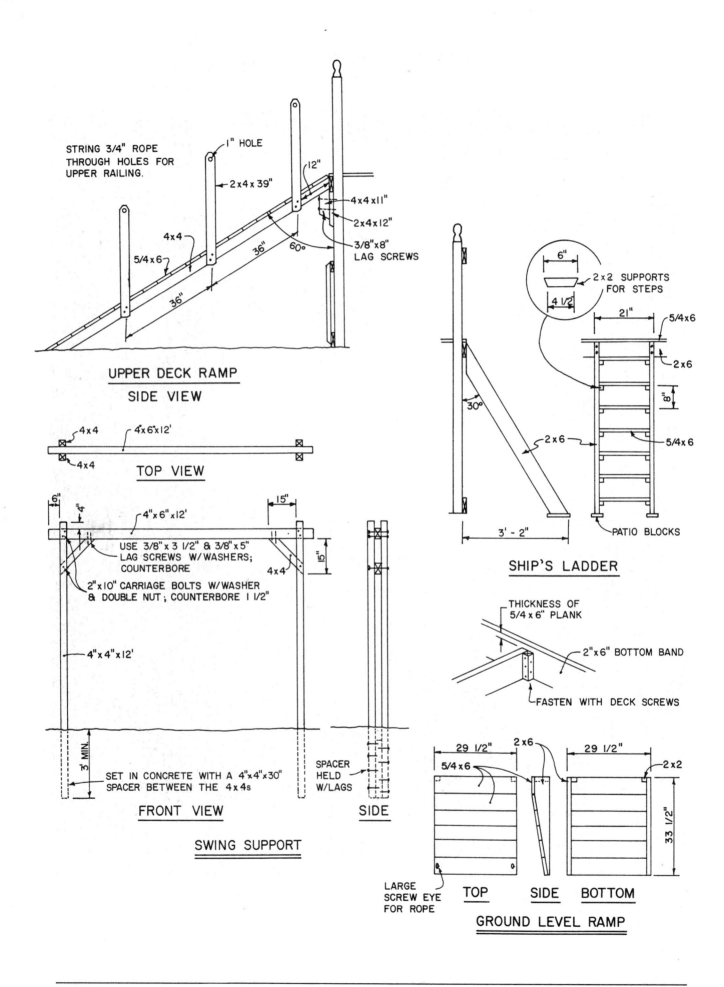

STRING 3/4" ROPE THROUGH HOLES FOR UPPER RAILING.

1" HOLE

2x4x39"

12"

4x4x11"

2x4x12"

3/8"x8" LAG SCREWS

4x4

5/4x6

36"

36"

60"

UPPER DECK RAMP
SIDE VIEW

4x4

4x6"x12'

4x4

TOP VIEW

6"

4"

4"x6"x12'

15"

USE 3/8" x 3 1/2" & 3/8"x 5" LAG SCREWS W/WASHERS; COUNTERBORE

4x4

2"x10" CARRIAGE BOLTS W/WASHER & DOUBLE NUT; COUNTERBORE 1 1/2"

4"x 4"x12'

3' MIN.

SET IN CONCRETE WITH A 4"x4"x30" SPACER BETWEEN THE 4 x 4s

SPACER HELD W/LAGS

FRONT VIEW   **SIDE**

SWING SUPPORT

2 x 2 SUPPORTS FOR STEPS

6"

4 1/2"

21"

5/4x6

2x6

8"

5/4x6

30°

2x6

3' - 2"

PATIO BLOCKS

SHIP'S LADDER

THICKNESS OF 5/4 x 6" PLANK

2"x6" BOTTOM BAND

FASTEN WITH DECK SCREWS

29 1/2"   2x6   29 1/2"

5/4x6

2x2

33 1/2"

LARGE SCREW EYE FOR ROPE

TOP   SIDE   BOTTOM

GROUND LEVEL RAMP

ALL-AMERICAN PLAY HOUSE

Designed by Dale Szarka

This All-American Play House is not quite finished yet, but the intended occupant is eager to try it out.

This play house—or "fort," as the boys will call it—is named the All-American Play House because it is what a majority of kids have in mind when Dad asks them what kind of play house they would like. Their specifications: up in the air so they can climb up and down, large enough to camp out in, with a roof and a porch. This basic 6' × 6' play house will suit them perfectly.

The plans here include a stairway with a railing, but there are a variety of other ways to get up and down: rope ladder, climbing rope, slide, fireman's pole, etc. Let your children help decide which method their play house will utilize. You could install one on each end of the porch.

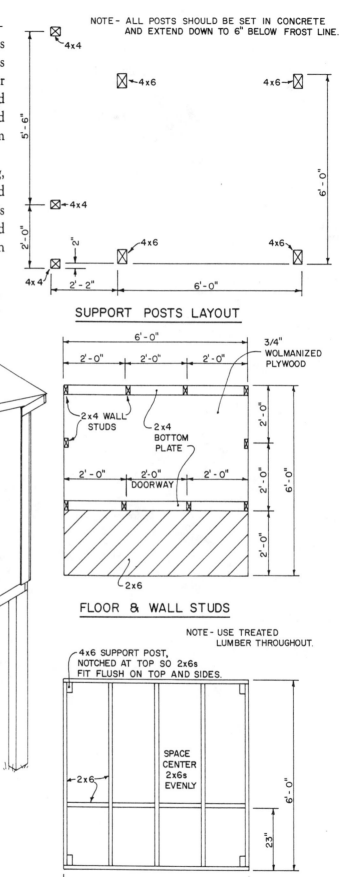

NOTE - ALL POSTS SHOULD BE SET IN CONCRETE AND EXTEND DOWN TO 6" BELOW FROST LINE.

SUPPORT POSTS LAYOUT

3/4" WOLMANIZED PLYWOOD

2x4 WALL STUDS

2x4 BOTTOM PLATE

DOORWAY

2x6

FLOOR & WALL STUDS

NOTE - USE TREATED LUMBER THROUGHOUT.

4x6 SUPPORT POST, NOTCHED AT TOP SO 2x6s FIT FLUSH ON TOP AND SIDES.

2x6

SPACE CENTER 2x6s EVENLY

FLOOR JOISTS

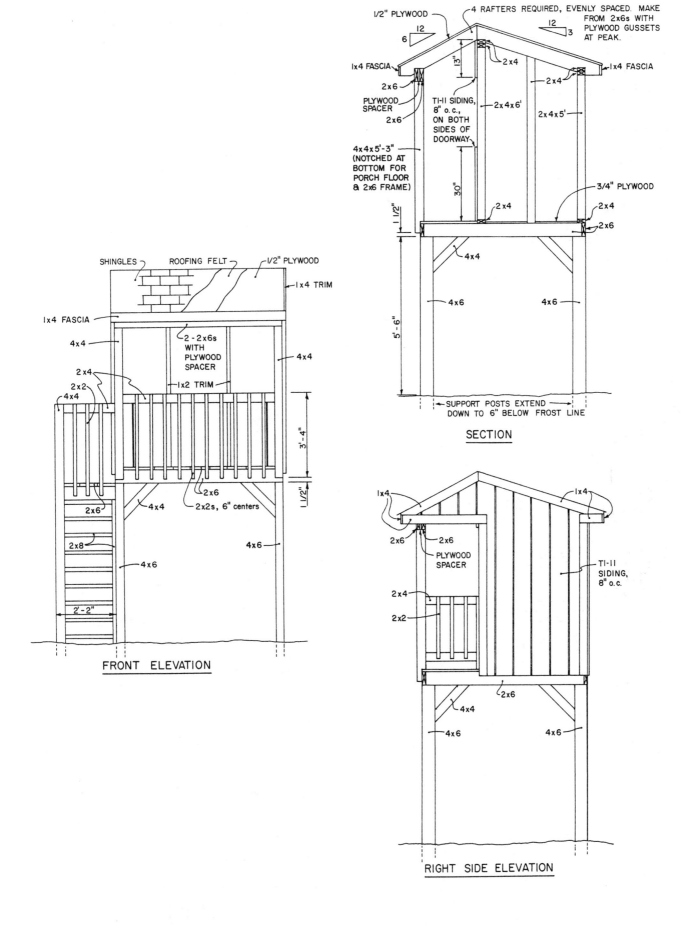

1/2" PLYWOOD

4 RAFTERS REQUIRED, EVENLY SPACED. MAKE
FROM 2x6s WITH
PLYWOOD GUSSETS
AT PEAK.

6 ⟋12   12⟍ 3

1x4 FASCIA   1x4 FASCIA
2x6   2x4
PLYWOOD   13"
SPACER   2x4
2x6   TI-11 SIDING,
             8" o.c.,   2x4x6'
             ON BOTH   2x4x5'
             SIDES OF
             DOORWAY
4x4x5'-3"   3/4" PLYWOOD
(NOTCHED AT
BOTTOM FOR   30"
PORCH FLOOR   2x4   2x4
& 2x6 FRAME)
1/2"   2x6
                              4x4

5'-6"   4x6   4x6

← SUPPORT POSTS EXTEND →
DOWN TO 6" BELOW FROST LINE

SECTION

SHINGLES   ROOFING FELT   1/2" PLYWOOD
                                              1x4 TRIM
1x4 FASCIA
4x4   2 - 2x6s
             WITH
             PLYWOOD   4x4
             SPACER
2x4   1x2 TRIM
2x2
4x4
                                              3'-4"
2x6
             2x6
2x8   2x2s, 6" centers   1 1/2"
             4x4
4x6   4x6

2'-2"

FRONT ELEVATION

1x4   1x4
2x6   2x6
PLYWOOD
SPACER   TI-11
2x4   SIDING,
2x2   8" o.c.

                   2x6
4x4
4x6   4x6

RIGHT SIDE ELEVATION

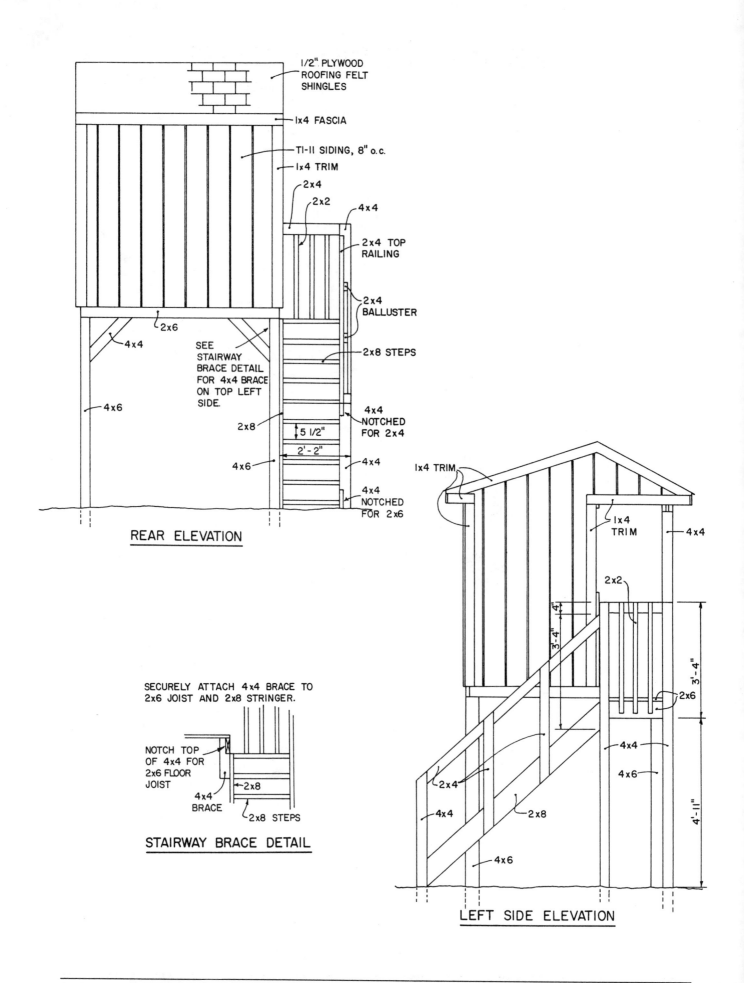

1/2" PLYWOOD
ROOFING FELT
SHINGLES

1x4 FASCIA

TI-11 SIDING, 8" o.c.

1x4 TRIM

2x4

2x2

4x4

2x4 TOP
RAILING

2x4
BALLUSTER

2x8 STEPS

2x6

4x4

SEE
STAIRWAY
BRACE DETAIL
FOR 4x4 BRACE
ON TOP LEFT
SIDE.

4x6

4x4
NOTCHED
FOR 2x4

2x8

5 1/2"

2' - 2"

4x6

4x4

4x4
NOTCHED
FOR 2x6

REAR ELEVATION

SECURELY ATTACH 4x4 BRACE TO
2x6 JOIST AND 2x8 STRINGER.

NOTCH TOP
OF 4x4 FOR
2x6 FLOOR
JOIST

4x4
BRACE

2x8

2x8 STEPS

STAIRWAY BRACE DETAIL

1x4 TRIM

1x4
TRIM

4x4

2x2

4"

3'-4"

3' - 4"

2x6

4x4

4x6

2x4

2x4

4x4

2x8

4'-11"

4x6

LEFT SIDE ELEVATION

THE GINGERBREAD HOUSE

Designed by Kathy Smith Anthenat

This adorable house for younger children isn't edible like the house Hansel and Gretel found in the woods, but it's every bit as cute and a lot more fun. The floor area is approximately 4′ × 5′; sloping side walls make the inside even roomier. There are five windows—at three different heights—and one 4½′ tall doorway. The roof peak is 7′ high.

NOTE - USE TREATED WOOD FOR ALL
WOOD IN THIS PLAYHOUSE.

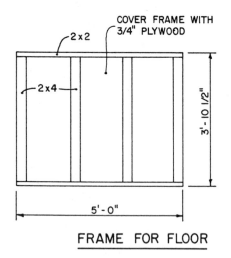

FRAME FOR FLOOR

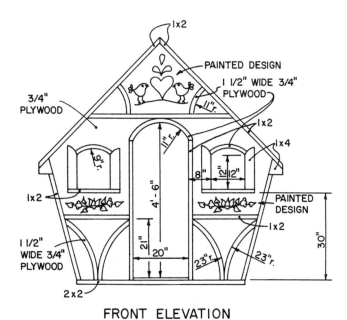

FRONT ELEVATION

FRONT WALL AND RAFTER
EXTERIOR VIEW

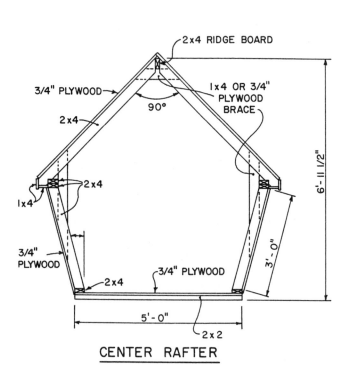

CENTER RAFTER

NOTE - ROOF SHOULD BE COVERED WITH
ROOFING FELT AND SHINGLES.

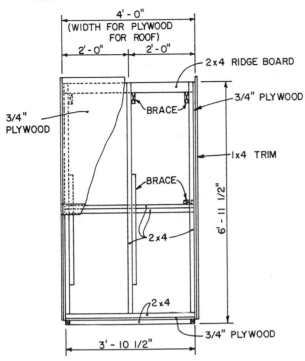

SIDE VIEW OF FRAMING

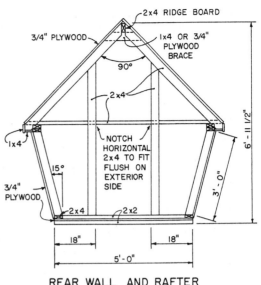

REAR WALL AND RAFTER
EXTERIOR VIEW

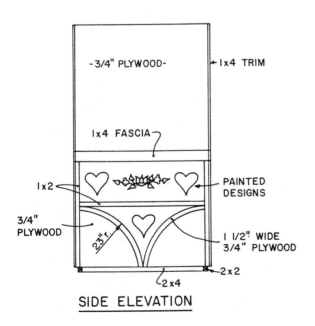

SIDE ELEVATION

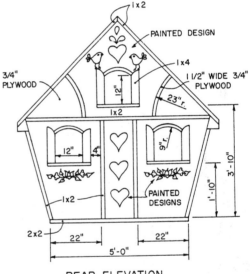

REAR ELEVATION

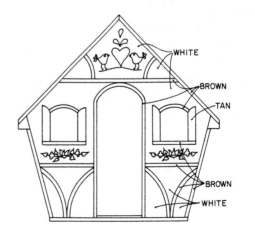

SUGGESTED COLOR SCHEME

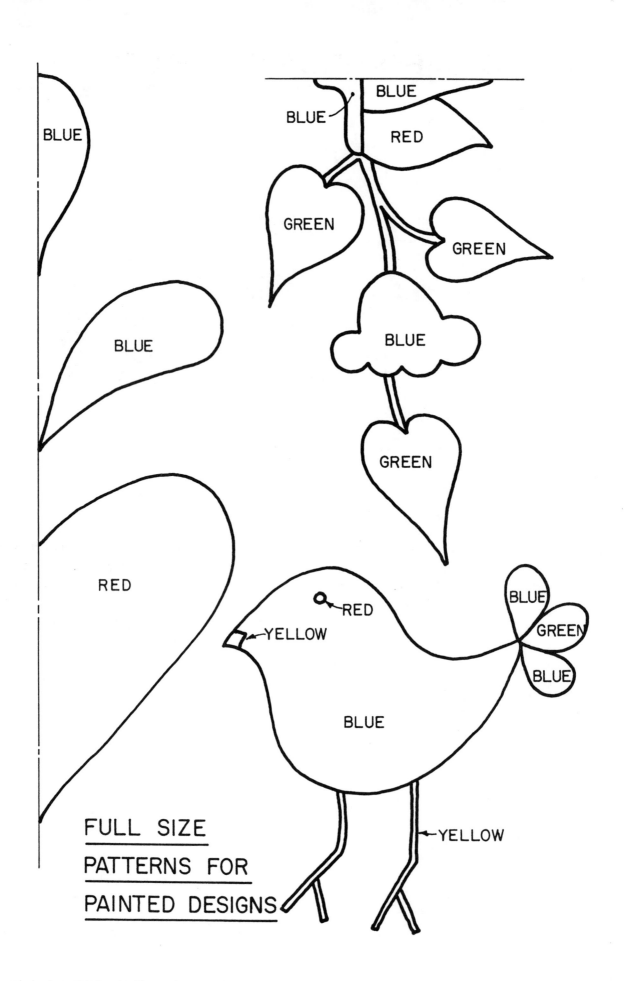

BLUE

BLUE
BLUE
RED

GREEN
GREEN

BLUE

GREEN

RED
BLUE

RED
YELLOW
BLUE
GREEN
BLUE
BLUE

FULL SIZE
PATTERNS FOR
PAINTED DESIGNS

YELLOW

CLUBHOUSE/GARDEN SHED

Courtesy of MacMillan Bloedel/Structural Board Association

Here's a shed designed with many uses in mind. Kids will love the privacy it affords them as a play house or the neighborhood clubhouse. Plant climbing vines to cover the trellis for a lovely shaded patio. Children will enjoy reading and playing games there, or use it for the wading pool, and you won't have to worry about it ruining a section of the lawn because it stayed in one spot too long. When play time is over, all the toys can be quickly stashed in the clubhouse for a clutter-free backyard. This 8' × 8' building is also ideal for gardening and lawn supplies, bicycles, etc.

BILL OF MATERIALS

Aspenite Panels

9 pieces	4 x 8 x $^1/_4$" (walls & roof)
2 pieces	4 x 8 x $^7/_{16}$" (floor) or $^3/_8$" plywood

Lumber

2 pieces	4 x 4—8' long—rough W.R. Cedar (sills)
11 pieces	2 x 4—8' long (joists & trimmers)
6 pieces	2 x 3—4' long (wall framing)
21 pieces	2 x 3—6' long (wall framing)
2 pieces	2 x 3—7' long (wall framing)
10 pieces	2 x 3—8' long (wall framing)
15 pieces	2 x 3—8' long (roof framing)
2 pieces	2 x 8—10' long (beam & cap)
4 pieces	1 x 3—6' long (corner trim)
2 pieces	1 x 4—4' long (trims, fascia & barge boards)
6 pieces	1 x 4—6' long (trims, fascia & barge boards)
4 pieces	1 x 4—8' long (trims, fascia & barge boards)
5 pieces	1 x 4—6' long (door framing, astragal, handles)
4 pieces	1 x 4—4' long (door framing, astragal, handles)
3 pieces	1 x 3—8' long (window framing)
6 pieces	1 x 2—8' long (window framing)
1 piece	1 x 4—8' long (below window trim)
1 piece	$^3/_8$ x 1 $^1/_4$—4' long (door stop moulding)
2 pieces	$^3/_4$ x $^3/_4$—3' long (nailing piece for Filon)
48 lineal feet	$^1/_2$ x $^1/_2$ (cove mould)
24 lineal feet	$^3/_8$ x 1 $^1/_4$ (window stop)

ALSO REQUIRED: 4 pieces PVC 26" x 72", 2 pieces Filon 26" x 84", 3 pr. 4" Tee-hinges (galvanized), 3 pr. 3" Butt hinges (galvanized), mastic bead, glass for windows, galvanized nails, special nails for PVC and Filon, deadbolts and latch, paint.

CONSTRUCTION STEPS
(read plans very carefully)

1. Prepare site. Position 4 x 4 cedar sills and level.

2. Assemble 2 x 4 joists 12" o.c. and nail to trimmers (above ground at least 2"). Apply $^7/_{16}$" Aspenite panels or plywood. NOTE: If $^3/_8$" plywood used, apply across the floor framing and add blocking under panel joins.

3. Assemble 2 x 3 roof frames in a similar manner.

4. Assemble studs & plates, etc., for front wall and nail together.

5. Apply ¼" Aspenite panel to front wall so top is flush with top of window blocking. Leave 4" overlap at base of wall. Frame windowless back wall and cover in the same way. Tip up into place and temporarily brace from outside.

6. Assemble studs & plates for side walls. Tip up (frames only) and align with front and back walls. Then nail corners together (see CORNER DETAIL, page 163).

7. Fasten cap and ledgers to the roof beam and install.

8. Place roof frames in position and nail in place.

9. Apply ¼" Aspenite panels to side walls.

10. Apply ¼" Aspenite panels to larger roof frame and then cover with PVC.

11. Apply fascia.

12. Apply Filon to smaller roof frame (see ROOF DETAIL, page 163).

13. Apply window frames and fit glass.

14. Fit, assemble, and install opening sash (see OPENING SASH DETAIL, page 163).

15. Assemble doors (2'0" x 5'-10 $^7/_8$" each), as shown. Apply astragal and pulls. Install doors & hardware (see DOOR BASE DETAIL, page 163).

16. Apply trim to corners, windows, etc., as shown, and suitable exterior paint finish. (If Trellis is desired, see TRELLIS DETAILS, page 163).

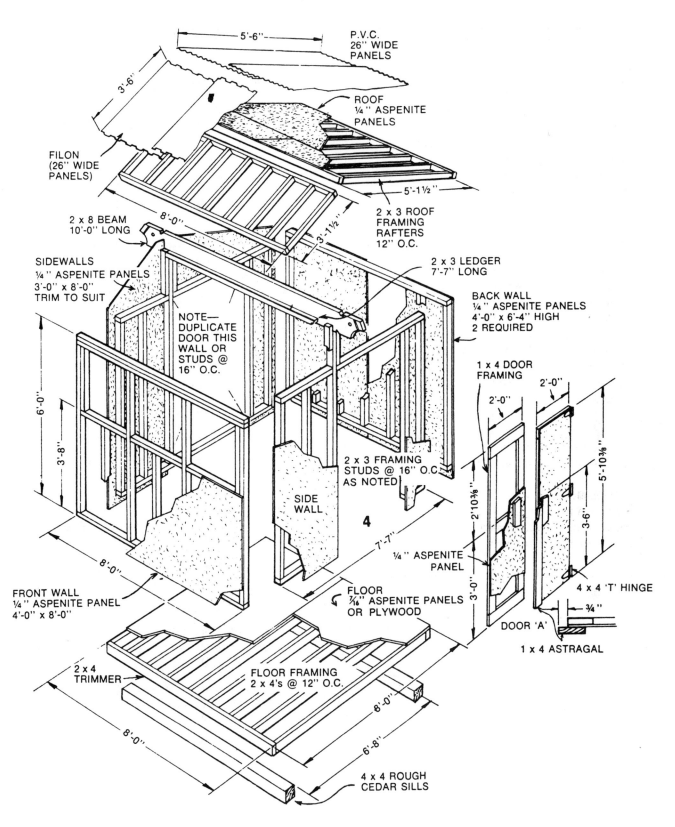

P.V.C. 26" WIDE PANELS

5'-6"

3'-6"

FILON (26" WIDE PANELS)

ROOF ¼" ASPENITE PANELS

5'-1½"

2 x 8 BEAM 10'-0" LONG

8'-0"

3-1½"

2 x 3 ROOF FRAMING RAFTERS 12" O.C.

2 x 3 LEDGER 7'-7" LONG

SIDEWALLS ¼" ASPENITE PANELS 3'-0" x 8'-0" TRIM TO SUIT

NOTE— DUPLICATE DOOR THIS WALL OR STUDS @ 16" O.C.

BACK WALL ¼" ASPENITE PANELS 4'-0" x 6'-4" HIGH 2 REQUIRED

6'-0"

3'-8"

2 x 3 FRAMING STUDS @ 16" O.C. AS NOTED

SIDE WALL

4

1 x 4 DOOR FRAMING

2'-0"

2'-0"

2'10⅜"

5'-10⅜"

3'-6"

¼" ASPENITE PANEL

3'-0"

4 x 4 'T' HINGE

7'-7"

DOOR 'A'

¾"

1 x 4 ASTRAGAL

8'-0"

FRONT WALL ¼" ASPENITE PANEL 4'-0" x 8'-0"

FLOOR ⅞" ASPENITE PANELS OR PLYWOOD

2 x 4 TRIMMER

FLOOR FRAMING 2 x 4's @ 12" O.C.

8'-0"

8'-0"

6'-8"

4 x 4 ROUGH CEDAR SILLS

NOTE: *FASTEN ASPENITE PANELS WITH 1½" GALVANIZED COMMON NAILS AT 6" CENTRES ON PANEL EDGES AND 12" CENTRES ON INTERMEDIATE FRAMES

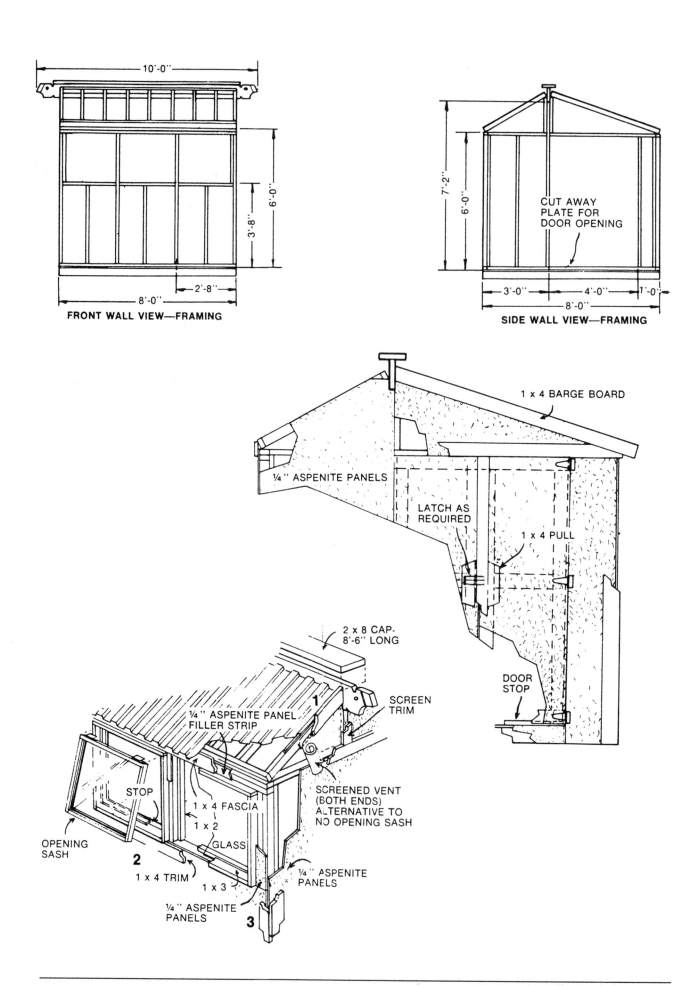

10'-0"

6'-0"

3'-8"

2'-8"

8'-0"

FRONT WALL VIEW—FRAMING

7'-2"

6'-0"

CUT AWAY
PLATE FOR
DOOR OPENING

3'-0" **4'-0"** **1'-0"**

8'-0"

SIDE WALL VIEW—FRAMING

1 x 4 BARGE BOARD

¼" ASPENITE PANELS

LATCH AS
REQUIRED

1 x 4 PULL

DOOR
STOP

2 x 8 CAP.
8'-6" LONG

¼" ASPENITE PANEL
FILLER STRIP

SCREEN
TRIM

STOP

SCREENED VENT
(BOTH ENDS)
ALTERNATIVE TO
NO OPENING SASH

1 x 4 FASCIA

1 x 2

GLASS

OPENING
SASH

1 x 4 TRIM

1 x 3

¼" ASPENITE
PANELS

¼" ASPENITE
PANELS

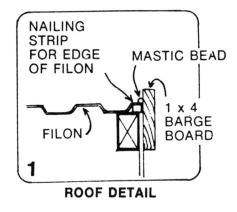

ROOF DETAIL

NAILING STRIP FOR EDGE OF FILON
MASTIC BEAD
1 x 4 BARGE BOARD
FILON
1

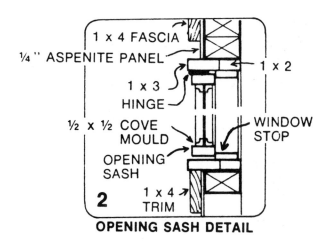

OPENING SASH DETAIL

1 x 4 FASCIA
¼ " ASPENITE PANEL
1 x 2
1 x 3
HINGE
½ x ½ COVE MOULD
WINDOW STOP
OPENING SASH
1 x 4 TRIM
2

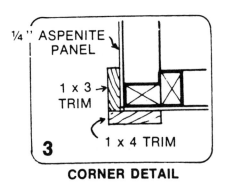

CORNER DETAIL

¼ " ASPENITE PANEL
1 x 3 TRIM
1 x 4 TRIM
3

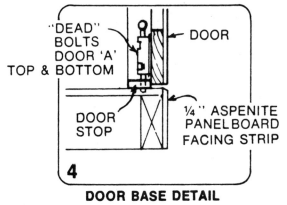

DOOR BASE DETAIL

"DEAD" BOLTS DOOR 'A' TOP & BOTTOM
DOOR
DOOR STOP
¼ " ASPENITE PANELBOARD FACING STRIP
4

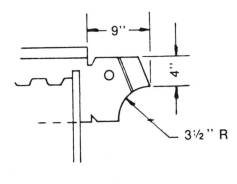

TRELLIS DETAIL

CUT AWAY TO CLEAR FILON
2 x 4 CEDAR
4 x 4 CEDAR
4 x 4 STEEL ANGLE

BEAM ENDS

9"
4"
3½" R

PART II

Play House Kit Manufacturers

HANDY HOME PRODUCTS

Handy Home Products
P.O. Box 548
Walled Lake, MI 48390
313-624-1010
800-221-1849
Fax 313-624-1082

Offers a line of ready-to-assemble wooden kits.

The Cedar Chalet

4' × 6' × 6' high; includes three window openings, flower box, pre-assembled door. Courtesy of Handy Home Products.

The Weekender Lodge

8' × 16' × 12' high; includes a domed skylight, three jalousie windows, two lofts. Courtesy of Handy Home Products.

Golden Carousel Cedar Sandbox

6' diameter × 7' high; all cedar. Courtesy of Handy Home Products.

The Sundowner

8' × 16' × 8' high; includes a single door between porch and storage area, double doors in the rear, two jalousie windows. Courtesy of Handy Home Products.

CHILDLIFE INC.

ChildLife Inc.
55 Whitney Street
Holliston, MA 01746
508-429-4639
Fax 508-429-3874

Offers indoor and outdoor play structure kits.

Quadro Kit

Sandcastle 4

Lightweight, indoor/outdoor construction kits to assemble and reassemble into a variety of play structures. Courtesy of ChildLife Inc.

One of many wood play structure designs offered. Requires a 19' × 14' space. Courtesy of ChildLife Inc.

LILLIPUT PLAY HOMES

Lilliput Play Homes
P.O. Box 533
Library, PA 15129-0533
412-831-2622

Offers several styles of play houses, including the two shown here. Also offers accessories to go with the play houses: ice cream table and chairs, rocker, etc.

The Victorian Mansion

8' long × 5' deep plus a 1' entrance. Tower is 7'6" high; roof is 6' high. Courtesy of Lilliput Play Homes.

The Olde Firehouse

8' long × 5' deep, with an 8'×3' loft; 8'2" high. Courtesy of Lilliput Play Homes.

SOUTHERN CYPRESS LOG HOMES

Southern Cypress Log Homes
Home Office:
P.O. Box 209
Crystal River, FL 32623
904-795-0777

Regional Office:
20495 Beals Chapel Road
Lenoir City, TN 37771
615-986-1074

The Creekstone

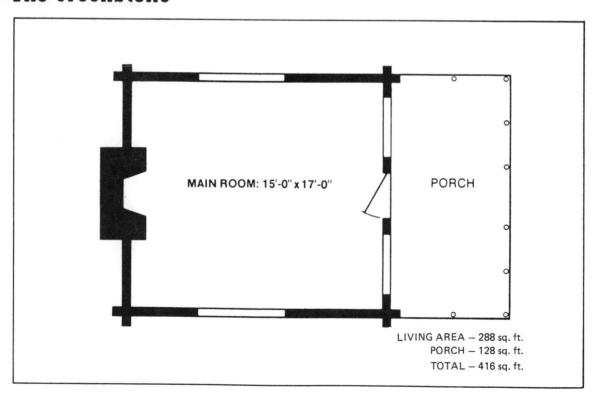

MAIN ROOM: 15'-0" x 17'-0"   PORCH

LIVING AREA — 288 sq. ft.
PORCH — 128 sq. ft.
TOTAL — 416 sq. ft.

CHILD DEVELOPMENT PLAY SYSTEMS

Child Development Play Systems
8089 Mayfield Road
Chesterland, OH 44026

Carries a complete line of playground equipment for residential and commercial use.

Rainbow Sunshine Castle

Rainbow Castle Climber IV

Courtesy of Child Development Play Systems.

Courtesy of Child Development Play Systems.

OREGON DOME, INC.

Oregon Dome, Inc.
3215 Meadow Lane
Eugene, OR 97402
503-689-3443
Fax 503-689-9275

This 23'6" Dome would make a spacious play house now and guest house later.

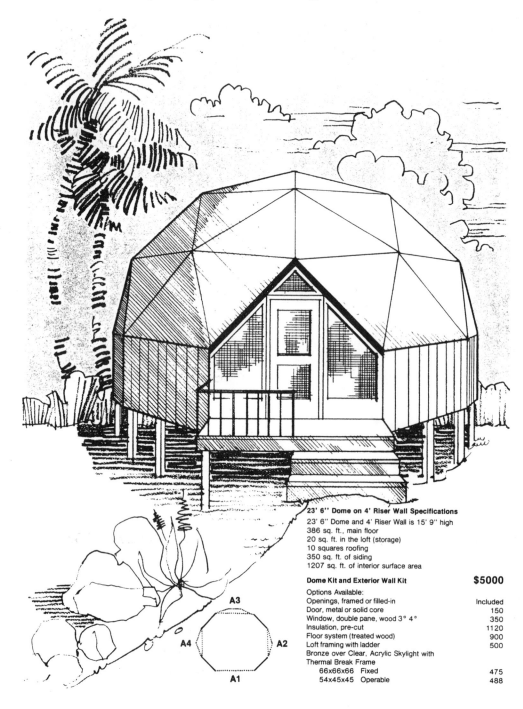

23' 6'' Dome on 4' Riser Wall Specifications

23' 6" Dome and 4' Riser Wall is 15' 9" high
386 sq. ft., main floor
20 sq. ft. in the loft (storage)
10 squares roofing
350 sq. ft. of siding
1207 sq. ft. of interior surface area

Dome Kit and Exterior Wall Kit	$5000
Options Available:	
Openings, framed or filled-in	Included
Door, metal or solid core	150
Window, double pane, wood 3° 4°	350
Insulation, pre-cut	1120
Floor system (treated wood)	900
Loft framing with ladder	500
Bronze over Clear, Acrylic Skylight with Thermal Break Frame	
66x66x66 Fixed	475
54x45x45 Operable	488

INDEX